Goodrich Castle

THE CASTLES

OF HEREFORDSHIRE

AND WORCESTERSHIRE

Mike Salter

FOLLY PUBLICATIONS

ACKNOWLEDGEMENTS

The photographs in this book were taken by the author between 1980 and 2000. He also prepared the maps and drew the plans. There are also a few old postcards reproduced from originals in the author's collection. Plans are mostly drawn to common scales of 1:800 and 1:2000, although a few buildings such as gatehouses and keeps are shown at 1:400. Thanks to Roger Stirling-Brown who supplied a lot of extra material for this extensively revised second edition.

AUTHOR'S NOTES

This series of books (see full list inside back cover) are intended as portable field guides giving as much information and illustrative material as possible in volumes of modest size, weight and price. As a whole the series gives a lot of information on lesser known sites. The aim in the castle books has been to mention, where the information is known to the author, owners or custodians of buildings who erected or altered parts of them, and those who were the first or last to hold an estate, an important office, or a title. Those in occupation at the time of dramatic events such as sieges are also sometimes named. Other owners and occupants whose lives had little effect on the condition of the buildings are generally not mentioned, nor are 19th or 20th century events or ghost stories, myths and legends.

The books are intended to be used in conjunction with the Ordnance Survey 1:50,000 scale maps. Grid references are given in the gazetteers together with a coding system indicating which buildings can be visited or easily seen by the public from adjacent public open spaces which is explained on page 88. Generally speaking, maps will be required to find some of the lesser known earthworks.

Each level of a building is called a storey in this book, the basement being the first or lowest storey with its floor near courtyard level unless mentioned as otherwise.

Measurements given in the text and scales on the plans are in metres, the unit used by the author for all measurements taken on site. Although the buildings were designed using feet the metric scales are much easier to use and are now standard amongst those studying historic buildings and ancient sites. For those who feel a need to make a conversion 3 metres as almost 10 feet. Unless specifically mentioned as otherwise all dimensions are external at or near ground level, but above the plinth if there is one. On plans the original work is shown black, post-1800 work is stippled and alterations and additions of intermediate periods are hatched.

ABOUT THE AUTHOR

Mike Salter is 47 and has been a professional writer and publisher since he went on the Government Enterprise Allowance Scheme for unemployed people in 1988. He is particularly interested in the planning and layout of medieval buildings and has a huge collection of plans of churches and castles he has measured during tours (mostly by bicycle and motorcycle) throughout all parts of the British Isles since 1968. Wolverhampton born and bred, Mike now lives in an old cottage beside the Malvern Hills. His other interests include walking, maps, railways, board games, morris dancing, playing percussion instruments and calling dances with a folk group.

Copyright 2000 Mike Salter. Original saddle-stitched first edition published Dec 1989. This extensively revised new edition with extra illustrations published Dec 2000. Folly Publications, Folly Cottage, 151 West Malvern Rd, Malvern, Worcs WR14 4AY Printed by Aspect Design, 89 Newtown Rd, Malvern, Worcs WR14 2PD

Gateway arches, Brampton Bryan

CONTENTS

Introduction to Herefordshire Castles   Page 4

Gazetteer of Herefordshire Castles   Page 12

List of Moated Sites in Herefordshire   Page 73

Introduction to Worcestershire Castles   Page 75

Gazetteer of Worcestershire Castles   Page 76

List of Moated Sites in Worcestershire   Page 87

Glossary of Terms   Page 88

Further Reading   Page 88

Access to the Sites   Page 88

Maps of the two counties appear inside the front cover.

INTRODUCTION TO HEREFORDSHIRE CASTLES

Before the Normans arrived in England in the mid 11th century all fortifications in what had by then become the county of Herefordshire were built by communities or the state. The concept of privately owned defensible residences does not appear to have been favoured by the Saxon nobles. In 1049 the defeat of Bishop Ealdred of Worcester by Gruffydd ap Rhydderch of South Wales prompted Ralph Mantes and his neighbours to build castles at Hereford, Ewyas Harold and Richard's Castle. Ralph, a nephew of King Edward the Confessor, was a Norman by birth and the new castles were regarded as novel and alien to English culture. Their existence caused friction at King Edward's court between his Norman friends and relations and the Anglo-Danish party led by Earl Godwin. The castle at Ewyas was destroyed in 1052 after Godwin and his sons returned from a brief period of exile, and when the Welsh sacked Hereford in 1055 it would appear that Godwin's son Harold, then holding the reins of government, concentrated on the refortification of the city rather than rebuilding the castle.

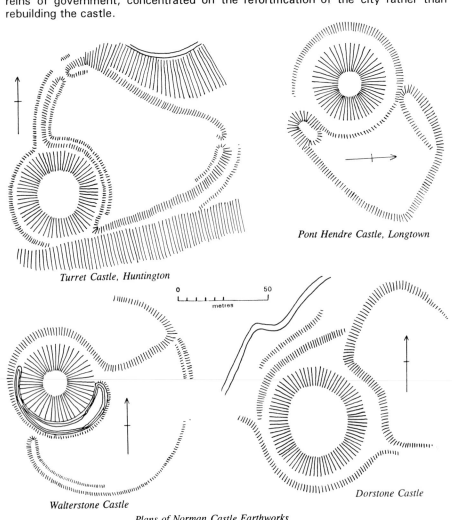

Pont Hendre Castle, Longtown

Turret Castle, Huntington

0   50
metres

Walterstone Castle

Dorstone Castle

Plans of Norman Castle Earthworks

In 1067 the newly crowned William I granted the earldom of Hereford to his cousin William Fitz-Osbern, said to be the ablest and bravest Norman in his army. He was granted an unusually compact group of estates with special powers to rule Herefordshire as one of a series of semi-independent earldoms forming a buffer-zone between the newly conquered English and the then unconquered Welsh. William Fitz-Osbern and other lords such as Roger de Lacy and Hugh de Mortimer and their knights formed a thin veneer of landowning, French-speaking Normans in a district populated by Saxons and vulnerable to Welsh attacks. They rapidly consolidated their uneasy hold on the county by filling it with castles built with the aid of slave labour. In four years, prior to being killed in Normandy in February 1071, William Fitz-Osbern rebuilt the castles of Ewyas Harold and Hereford, and built new castles at Clifford and Wigmore, plus three more in Monmouthshire. The great lords gave units of land called manors to their knights in return for specified periods of military service, which often included castle garrison duty, this system being known as feudalism.

On a rocky site at Chepstow in Monmouthshire unsuited for the creation of earthworks William Fitz-Osbern built a stone keep containing a hall over a low basement and two stone walled courts, but all the early castles in Herefordshire were not built of mortared stone, but of earth and wood. These were quicker and easier materials to work with and in any case there was a comparative lack of stone masons since the Saxons built most of their houses and some of their churches of wood. The usual form of early castles was for the lord's house or tower to be raised within a small palisaded court on a high earthen mound or motte surrounded by a ditch. On one side would lie a larger, lower court called a bailey, defended by a rampart with a palisade and ditch, and containing a hall, chapel, workshops, stables, granary, and sundry farm buildings, all timber framed with roofs of shingles or thatch. The basic design varied according to the terrain and the resources available. An enclosure with a high rampart (now known as a ringwork) was sometimes provided instead of a motte, and baileys were omitted or duplicated and made whatever size and shape local circumstances dictated. Natural landscape features were utilised where possible, hillocks and spurs being shaped and heightened into steep-sided and level-topped mottes. The Welsh Border counties contain the highest concentration of motte and bailey castles in Britain and there are over ninety of them in Herefordshire. The earthworks of many of them are small and worn-down, but there are fine earthworks remaining at Clifford, Ewyas Harold, Richard's Castle, and Wigmore which are all mentioned in Domesday Book, King William's land ownership survey of 1086.

Timber is vulnerable to accidental or deliberate destruction by fire and eventually rots away when in constant contact with damp soil. Although structures of timber remained an important element in the defences of most castles up until the 14th century the most important parts would gradually be replaced by walls and towers of mortared stone. Few of the stone structures can be closely dated either by documentation or architectural or archaeological evidence but it does not appear that any of the castles of Herefordshire possessed stone defences before the middle of the 12th century. Remnants of buildings which can be dated with certainty before 1200 are few. Goodrich has a small square tower keep of c1150-70 containing a hall and chamber over a basement. The lower part of an octagonal tower keep remains on the motte at Richard's Castle. At Kilpeck are fragments of an enclosing wall upon the summit of the large motte. In modern parlance this is a shell keep, although the word keep is no older than the 16th century, the words donjon or turris (tower) being used in the medieval period. Most of the shell keep at Wigmore seems to be 14th century, but there are foundations of another early example at Llancillo and slight traces exist of several others. Small square towers seem to have stood on the mounds at Downton and Bredwardine. Nothing now remains of the large rectangular keep and the bailey walls which existed at Hereford by the year 1200.

The chapel at Goodrich before restoration

King Stephen campaigned in Herefordshire in 1138-9 but the county was held throughout his reign by the supporters of his rival the Empress Matilda, daughter of Henry I. In 1141 she created a new earldom of Hereford for Miles of Gloucester. His son Roger and Hugh de Mortimer and Gilbert de Lacy were the chief barons of Herefordshire when Matilda's son became king as Henry II in 1154. Other families which came into prominence were the Bohuns, for whom King John created a new earldom of Hereford in 1199, and the de Braose family, who were all-powerful in the southern part of the Welsh Marches until they fell out with King John in 1208.

The 13th century is the most notable period for stone castles in Herefordshire. Of c1200-20 are the unusual elongated polygonal keep at Snodhill which contained just a hall over a low basement, and the hall-block with a tall round tower at one corner within a rectangular moated platform at Pembridge. Although sometimes described as a keep the tower is smaller than other circular keeps. The round tower keep on the motte and the fragmentary bailey walls at Longtown are now regarded as the work of Walter de Lacy c1216-23, when he was sheriff of the county and its most powerful baron. Lyonshall has the base of another round tower keep built in the 1220s by one of de Lacy's knights, whilst a third is thought to have been built on the mound at Huntington by the de Braose family c1216-25, and another may have been built at Moccas in the 1290s. By c1220-45 Goodrich had a small rectangular court and in the same period small polygonal courts were built on the mound summits at Clifford, Ewyas Harold and Hereford. In each case there were round flanking towers, and these were also provided at the rather larger enclosure of this period at Weobley, where there was also a large rectangular keep with round corner towers, a plan repeated in several 13th century Irish keeps, but (except for a small tower at Rye) not paralleled in England until a keep like it was built at Dudley c1307-20. With the demise of the main line of the de Lacy family in 1241 the Mortimers and Bohuns remained all-powerful in Herefordshire throughout the 13th and 14th centuries. They took opposing sides in the conflicts of the 1260s between Henry III and his barons but both opposed Edward II.

The keep at Goodrich

The keep at Pembridge

In the period c1270-1300 the curtain walls, turrets and twin-towered gatehouse at Pembridge were erected, and the old earthworks at Wilton were modified to take a rectangular courtyard with round and polygonal flanking towers. In grandeur but not overall scale both are eclipsed by the splendid new works of the earls of Pembroke at Goodrich, producing a building of advanced design which combined great defensive strength with stately apartments. The chambers are set around a small court and are constructed as integral units with the new curtain walls. At one corner is a large gatehouse containing a chapel and other fine rooms, whilst further chambers are contained within large round towers rising from square bases set at the other three corners. Despite its ruined state, Goodrich is by far the most interesting and best preserved castle in Herefordshire. Only there and at Wilton do medieval domestic apartments survive in an understandable condition.

The Mortimers' chief seat at Wigmore as rebuilt in the early 14th century comprised a large bailey with various rectangular towers, an oval shell keep with apartments at the far end, and a palatial set of apartments, of which little remains, set on a shelf below the keep but above the bailey. The outer ward protecting two sides of the inner ward at Goodrich and containing stables is also early 14th century, whilst the towers added to the bailey wall at Snodhill may be of the 1360s.

As times became more peaceful after Edward I's final defeat of the Welsh in the early 1280s there was less need for massive and expensive fortifications, but military features were often retained as symbols of the lordly rank of the owner of a house and as a measure of protection against unruly neighbours or rebellious peasants. An early example of a lightly fortified manor house was Ashperton, for which a licence to crenellate was granted by Edward I in 1296, although only the moat now remains. Since Richard I's reign the building of fortifications was carefully controlled by the crown and favoured courtiers and loyal servants were rewarded by licences to crenellate (embattle) their residences. Parts of the hall and gateway remain of an early 14th century mansion at Brampton Bryan. These parts occupied most of two ranges set on either side of a tiny court. Other ranges with apartments and service rooms would have occupied the other two sides. There was a moat but no flanking towers, but later in the 14th century a barbican with two round towers was added in front of the gateway, more to impress visitors than for serious defence. Little now remains of the contemporary castle at Penyard, probably with a similar layout.

Kentchurch Court has a keep-like corner tower, a hall range and a gatehouse remaining from a late 14th century courtyard mansion, whilst Hampton Court has a large gatehouse and corner turrets, being licensed in 1431. The castles of Bronsil, licensed in 1449 and 1460, Croft, probably of the 1470s but possibly somewhat earlier, and Treago as rebuilt in the 1490s all had corner towers, gatehouses and four ranges of apartments set around central courts. In each case a moat formed the primary defensive feature, although the towers at Treago have loops for handguns. This building was so small that it was later possible to roof over its central court. During the 15th century the Bohun estates passed to the Stafford family and the Mortimer lands passed to Richard, Duke of York, becoming his power base in his struggles against the Lancastrian Henry VI in the 1450s. Further details about these families and also those of Baskerville, Beauchamp, Chandos, Clifford, Devereaux, Grey, Harley, Pembridge, Say, Solaris, Talbot, and Verdon, among others, plus some of the Bishops of Hereford, can be found amongst the gazetteer entries.

Gatehouse at Hampton Court

Interior of the keep at Longtown

In the medieval period castle walls of rubble were often limewashed both inside and out, making them look very different to the way they appear today. Dressed stones around windows and doorway would be left uncovered. Domestic rooms would have had murals of biblical, historical or heroic scenes mostly painted in red, yellow and black. Wall hangings decorated with the same themes or heraldry gradually became more common from the 14th century onwards. Although used in churches, glass was expensive and uncommon in secular buildings before the 15th century, so windows were originally closed with wooden shutters. As a result rooms were dark when the weather was too cold or wet for them to be opened for light and ventilation. Large openings in the outer walls sometimes had bars or projecting grilles even if high above ground level. Living rooms usually had fireplaces although some halls had central hearths with the smoke escaping through louvres in the roof. Latrines were common, although often only their outlet shoots now remain.

Furnishings were sparse up until the 15th century although the embrasures of upper storey windows sometimes have built-in stone seats, as at Goodrich. Lords with several castles tended to circulate around them administering their manorial courts and consuming agricultural produce on the spot. Seats belonging to great lords could be left almost empty when they were not in residence. For much of their lives castles gradually crumbled away with only a skeleton staff to administer the estates. When Owain Glyndwr rebelled against Henry IV in the early 1400s it was necessary for the king to order many of the decayed Welsh Marcher castles to be repaired, munitioned and garrisoned by their absentee lords. Servants travelled with their lords and sometimes also portable furnishings such as rugs, wall hangings, cooking vessels and bedding, all kept in wooden chests. The lord and his immediate family plus honoured guests and senior household officials would enjoy a fair degree of privacy by the late 13th century, having their own rooms. Servants and retainers enjoyed less comfort and privacy, sharing of beds and communal sleeping in any places that were warm being common.

Scattered across Herefordshire, but more numerous in the east half of the county, where there are less mottes, are platforms surrounded by moats which mark the sites of former medieval manor houses, most of which were not otherwise fortified. In many cases the original internal buildings were of perishable materials. The timber-framed 14th century house and 15th century gatehouse at Brockhampton was probably typical of these structures. Excavation of the platform at Breinton, however, exposed the foundations of a 12th century stone hall block with a thin surrounding curtain wall. The site is thought to have served as the vicarage for about a century. Most of the moats date from the 13th and 14th centuries, the most common form being a water-filled ditch about 10m wide and up to 3m deep surrounding a roughly rectangular platform from 40m to 60m long. The few moats with round platforms like that at Edwin Ralph may represent an earlier type transitional from mottes with higher but usually smaller summits. Earthworks like that at Dilwyn could be classed as either a defensible ringwork or a purely domestic moated site. Few Herefordshire moats have been excavated or properly surveyed so details about their history and true purpose in many cases can only by surmised.

The digging of ditches was not regulated like the construction of embattled walls but as only the gentry and wealthier clerics could obtain the labour needed to create them, moats were status symbols. They were not necessarily defensive in a military sense. They would serve to keep out vagrants and wild animals and keep in the children, servants and domestic animals of a household. They have always been valued as scenic features and formed a habitat for fish, eels and water fowl, which together formed a substantial part of the diet of the landed classes.

Fragment of keep at Snodhill   *Curtain wall at Longtown*

As a result of special powers being granted to various barons to create centres of military power to keep the Welsh in check, most of western Herefordshire formed parts of Marcher lordships in which royal officials had little power. This situation soon became an embarrassment and danger to the Crown, for the lords insisted on independence when the Welsh were weak and divided, but they called out for royal support when the Welsh united behind a single ruler and became a danger. Despite the Welsh defeat of the 1280s making them anachronistic, the special March lordships survived until abolished by Henry VIII in 1536. Clifford, Eardisley, Ewyas Harold, Ewyas Lacy (Longtown), Huntington, Witney, Wigmore and Winforton then became part of Herefordshire whilst Michaelchurch and Radnor were lost to the newly created county of Radnor. Many of the medieval lordly families had died out or lost their main seats by then and other families such as the Coningsbys, Cornewalls, and Scudamores had risen to take their place as Members of Parliament, Justices of the Peace, and leaders of the militia. At that time Henry VIII's topographer John Leyland travelled through Herefordshire and reported that many of the castles were decayed or totally ruined. Apart from the more recent fortified manor houses, which were probably all still in use, only the castles of Eardisley, Goodrich, Pembridge, Wigmore and Wilton seem to have still been inhabited by their owners or close relatives. Pembridge and Wilton have remains of new domestic accommodation of the 16th and 17th centuries, but the superior apartments at Goodrich remained adequate throughout this period without significant alterations or additions.

Treago Castle from the south

When civil war broke out between King Charles I and Parliament in 1642 the Herefordshire gentry mostly supported the king except for the Harleys of Brampton Bryan. Some castles were hastily patched up and garrisoned, but others, notably Wigmore, were dismantled to prevent the opposing side occupying them. The city of Hereford was occupied by Parliamentary troops for part of 1642 and 1643, and was attacked by a Scottish army under the Earl of Leven in August 1645, but it was only after the city fell to a surprise attack by Colonel Birch in December 1645 that the king's cause in the county was lost. It was then just a matter of time before the many lesser Royalist garrisons submitted, the last being Goodrich, which held out until the end of July 1646. All the castles then still regarded as tenable were slighted, except for that at Hereford which was demolished a few years later. Dismantled castles provided a convenient supply of valuable materials for other buildings throughout the 17th and 18th centuries, leaving little for us to study now.

The mansions of Hampton Court and Treago, which were not strong enough to stand up to 17th century cannon, appear to have survived the Civil War intact. Croft Castle was soon repaired and re-occupied, only to be drastically remodelled in the 18th century. Kentchurch Court also survives in a habitable but much altered state. A house was later built into the ruins at Wilton, and Pembridge was rebuilt in the late 17th century and again in the early 20th century. All the other buildings are ruins or are reduced to earthworks or just the buried footings of former stone walls.

The shell keep at Wigmore

GAZETTEER OF CASTLES IN HEREFORDSHIRE

ALMELEY CASTLE   SO 332514   F

During the 20th century the churchyard encroached upon the filled-in ditch of the NE side of the quadrangular bailey measuring about 50m across each way. on the south side is a motte rising about 8m high to a summit 11m in diameter. The bailey would have been difficult to defend after the church was provided with a west tower c1200 yet the site remained in use, William Cantilupe being constable in 1216, and Henry III receiving the homage of Simon de Montfort here in 1231, whilst Roger Pychard was in occupation in 1242. The fall of a tree on the mound a few years ago revealed what looked like part of the base of a round tower keep.

ASHPERTON CASTLE   SO 642415

In 1292 Edward I licensed the Burgundian William de Grandison to crenellate his house here. It later passed to the Milburnes and then to the Minningtons. All remains of the buildings had vanished by the 18th century when the site was planted with trees. An oval platform 58m from north to south by 45m wide is surrounded by a wet moat which opens out almost to a square and is crossed by a causeway on the east. There are slight traces of a rectangular outer court around the church to the east.

ASHTON MOTTE & CASTLE   SO 514650 & 517642

North of the village is a mound 6m high on one side overlooking a stream. SE of the village is the site of what is thought to have been a later medieval fortified house. It has a platform 1m high with upon it a rectangular mound 1m high and 30m square plus a round mound 14m in diameter and 1m high.

Almeley Motte

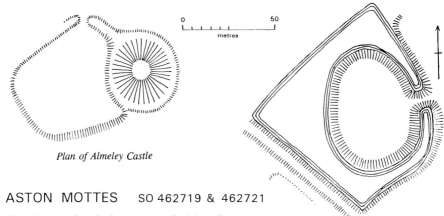

0   50
metres

Plan of Almeley Castle

ASTON MOTTES   SO 462719 & 462721

NE of the church is a mound rising 7m to a summit 21m in diameter. About 200m to the north is a second mound 3m high with traces of what appears to be a small bailey platform to the west.

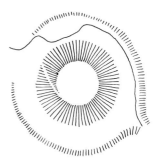

Plan of Ashperton Castle

BACTON CASTLE   SO 371335

At Newcourt Farm are buried footings of the castle of the de Bacton family, originally tenants of the de Lacys. A wall 1.8m thick surrounded a triangular court with buildings against the 33m long west side which seems to have been terminated by a square tower at the north end and a round tower at the south end. The east corner was filled by a round tower keep 10m in diameter with an apsidal projection towards the field. The ground falls away to the south and NE, and there is a ditch to the west, where there seems to have been a central gateway with a hall north of it.

Plan of Aston Motte

BIRTLEY CASTLE   SO 368694

In the garden of a house is a mound with scarps on three sides and pools to the west and south, whilst the curved bank south of the road formerly with a pool in front would be a relic of a bailey.

BOSBURY PALACE   SO 695436   V

Old Court Farmhouse is a former residence of the Bishops of Hereford, who held the manor until the late 17th century. Here Bishop Swinfield died in 1316. The site was enclosed by the River Leadon on the north and west and had a moat on the other two sides. On the east side is a much altered gatehouse of stone and timber, whilst the farmhouse includes 15th century work.

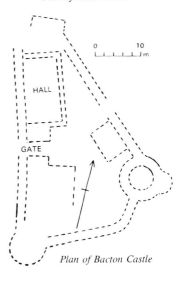

0   10
m

HALL

GATE

Plan of Bacton Castle

BRAMPTON BRYAN CASTLE   SO 369726

In the reign of Henry I Bernard Unspec, Lord of Kinlet in Shropshire, took the surname de Brampton from the estate he held here from the Mortimers in return for castle-guard service at their seat nearby at Wigmore. The Brampton Bryan site is of strategic importance, with traces of a Roman fortlet nearby, and it is assumed that Bernard erected a castle here. There was certainly a tower (perhaps of wood) and a curtilage here in 1293, when a survey of Bryan de Brampton estates was made after his death. The property passed via an heiress, Margaret, to Robert Harley, who built a mansion on the earlier earthworks with a hall and gatehouse on either side of a narrow court and presumably further ranges on the other two sides. A wide wet moat would have been the chief defensive feature. The imposing outer part of the gatehouse with round towers set on either side of the outer portal is thought to have been added slightly later in the 14th century by Bryan de Harley, probably in imitation of the outer gateway at Clifford Castle. Thus strengthened (and made a lot more impressive to look at) the castle was sucessfully held against Owain Glyndwr in 1403.

In the spring of 1642 Sir Robert Harley fortified the mansion for Parliament, leaving his wife Brilliana in charge whilst he was away in London. The surrounding district was then held by Royalists and in July 1643 the castle was besieged by Sir William Vavasour, governor of Hereford. Lady Harley and her force of about 100 men put up a brave defence until the Royalists withdrew their remaining forces from the blockade in September, Vavasour and some of his men having already gone off to help King Charles besiege Gloucester. Bombardment from a cannon mounted on the former tower of the church so damaged the castle roof that it was said none of the rooms remained dry. Lady Harley died from the stresses of the siege shortly afterwards and it was the family Doctor Nathan Wright who commanded the 60 men that vigorously resisted attacks by Sir Michael Woodhouse for three weeks until the garrison surrendered in April 1644. The walls are said to have been battered down to the ground, leaving only cellars, but this is clearly something of an exaggeration. In 1661 a new mansion was constructed alongside the wreck of the old one by Sir Edward Harley and the Harleys still reside within this much altered structure. It incorporates older features, which are either reset or are in situ remnants of a secondary court which would have presumably contained the stables and other outbuildings. One writer has suggested that the present mansion marks the site of the original inner court and that the present ruins are merely a late 17th century garden ornament built out of the 14th and 16th century materials of the destroyed castle, but there is a report that chambers above the castle gateway remained in use until damaged by a storm in the mid 18th century. Also the Buck brothers engraving of 1731 shows rather more of the castle than survives today.

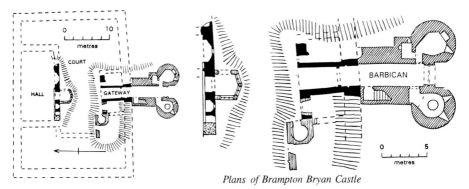

Plans of Brampton Bryan Castle

Brampton Bryan Castle

Only the south wall remains of the 14th century hall range. It contains the entrance doorway, now covered by a late 16th century porch, which led into the screened-off service passage at the east end of the room, which was about 7m wide. Set on either side of the doorway are contemporary loops, the eastern of which lighted the solar or a room below it. The original gatehouse was a three storey building lying only 9m south of the hall across what was probably once a cobbled court. The gatehouse measured about 9.2m by 5.4m externally and had guard rooms on either side of a passageway 2m wide and two large, pleasant rooms above. The north wall survives almost to the full height and has two windows and a fireplace remaining of the room over the passage, plus a top storey window, but the end walls have gone and little remains of the thicker south wall which formed part of the main south curtain wall. The outer portal has ballflower ornamentation, a typical motif of the early 14th century. The staircase turret adjoining the NW corner was added in the late 16th century when the adjoining apartments were rebuilt.

The slightly later barbican or outer part of the gatehouse more than doubled the length of the entrance passage and closed it with a second portcullis. On the west side is a straight stair to the upper storey rooms and on the east side is a projection containing a latrine. The towers are 4.6m in diameter and contain circular and polygonal rooms with narrow loops and single light windows with trefoiled-heads. Both towers retain their parapets. The castle earthworks have dramatically changed since the Civil War period, the moats having been filled in and much of the 3m high platform on which the castle stood having been cut away.

Hall block at Brampton Bryan

BREDWARDINE CASTLE   SO 335444 & 336440   F

Bredwardine was held by John de Bredwardine in the late 11th century. The Baskervilles held a castle here in 1227 with the Bohuns as their overlords. There is no mention of a castle in an estate inventory of 1374 at about which time Bredwardine passed by marriage to the Fouleshurst family of Cheshire. On the death of William Fouleshurst in 1439 Bredwardine passed back to Sir John Baskerville, who lived at Eardisley, a survey having described Bredwardine as waste and of no value.

The earthworks and buried foundations lying beside the west bank of the River Wye immediately south of the church look like a bailey with a low motte at the south end. Here probably stood the mansion erected or rebuilt by Roger Vaughan in 1639-40. It passed to the Cornewall family and was dismantled stone from it being taken to Moccas Court in 1775-81. However it seems that in the 12th century a stronghold stood on the platform beyond the fishponds to the south. Excavations there revealed traces of two phases of timber buildings and three phases of stone buildings, including a square tower, so it was probably the site of the castle mentioned in 1227, although in later years only a modest farmhouse stood on the site. A third site around here is the moat beyond the 14th century Old Court 0.3km north of the church.

BREINTON MOAT SO 473395

Excavations from 1959 to 1962 at the moated enclosure SW of the church revealed the footings of the southern part of a two storey hall block with a latrine turret at the SE corner. The platform was enclosed by a wall 1.5m thick with a gatehouse on the north side and evidence was found for timber buildings on the south side. The site was occupied from c1150 until part of the hall block collapsed in the 13th century. It may have served as the vicarage or was the seat of one of the knights owing service to the Bishop of Hereford.

BRILLEY MOTTE SO 273488

The bluff overlooking a dingle 1km SE of the church may be the site of a worn down motte and bailey castle. There is a mound 5m high at Cwmma Farm, 3km to the NE of the church at SO 276514. A stream probably fed a wet moat.

BRIDGE SOLLERS CASTLE SO 414426

The 17th century Knapp Farm appears to lie on the site of a bailey of a castle which guarded the ford replaced by the present bridge carrying the A438 in 1896. The main road probably runs through the site of a second bailey. The small motte shows signs of having had a stone building upon it.

BRINSOP COURT SO 446458

Brinsop belonged to the Tirrells in the 13th and 14th centuries and passed to the Dauncey family in the 15th century. The overgrown moated site at SO 446456 not far south of Brinsop Court may be the site of the Tirrells original house. The existing 14th century building has four ranges around a court and is also moated. It is of sandstone but there is much half-timbering, including an east range of 1913, and work of the 16th century and c1700 on the west. The south range contains an upper floor hall with a king-post roof. It is reached by external steps and has ogival-headed windows with reticulated tracery, with seats in the embrasures. The north range has small two-light windows with sunk-quadrant mouldings.

Plan of Breinton Moat

Brinsop Court

BRONSIL CASTLE   SO 749372

Richard, 2nd Lord Beauchamp of Powick, High Treasurer to Henry VI, was licensed in 1449 and 1460 to crenellate his manor house at Bronsil. On the death of his son John, 3rd Lord Beauchamp in 1496 Bronsil passed by marriage to the Reeds of Lugwardine. In the late 16th century they were troubled by a ghost that was only pacified when some bones belonging to John, 1st Lord Beauchamp, were sent over from Italy, where he had died, to be kept in the castle. It is said to have been burnt during the Civil War and although most of the outer walls are shown as still standing in the Buck brothers' print of 1731, only one tower still stood by 1779. By then the estate had been sold to Thomas Somers-Cocks, who lived in the former mansion of the Clinton family close to where the 1st Lord Somers erected a large new castellated mansion called Eastnor Castle in 1815. The site at Bronsil comprises a platform about 36m square, now overgrown with bushes and trees, surrounded by a wet moat with a slightly irregular layout on the west. On this side is a bridge to a gateway flanked by polygonal towers about 4.5m across over walls 1m thick. Part of the northern tower stood 10m high until it collapsed into the moat in 1991, the only other higher part being a stair turret on the NE. Footings around the other parts of the site indicate towers set at the corners and in the middle of each of the other three sides. The hall was probably in the east range with apartments and service rooms set within the north and south ranges, there being a central court about 18m across. There are indications of a concentric outer moat, now drained, on the east and south.

Bronsil Castle as it was in 1731

BUCKTON MOTTE

SO 383733

Buckton Farm may lie on the bailey of the adjacent 4m high mound. Two small mounds 3m high lie 1.5km to the north at SO 394741, east of the village of Leintwardine.

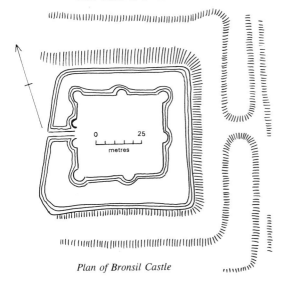

Plan of Bronsil Castle

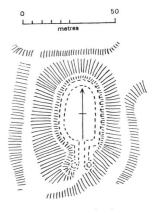

Plan of Byton Castle

Plan of Camp Wood Motte

Plan of Chanstone Motte

The last fragment of Bronsil Castle before collapse

BYTON CASTLE   SO 372642

Just south of the church is a mound with traces of an oval shell keep with at the south end evidence of a gatehouse with small twin full-round towers like those at Brampton Bryan, Clifford and Snodhill.

CABAL TUMP   SO 345585

A rectangular mound rises 4m above a ditch to a summit 22m by 18m. On the south is a bailey with traces of stonework. From the finds made when a trench was cut into the mound in 1874 it appears the site was later used as a pottery kiln.

CAMP WOOD MOTTE   SO 396654

Hugh Mortimer is thought to have built this motte 3km west of Aymestry church in the mid 12th century. It rises 5m above a ditch 3m deep and has an embanked summit. The bailey has been mostly ploughed-out.

CASTLE FROME   SO 671458

On a strong site on the end of a ridge high above the Norman church is a ringwork 4m high and 45m across with traces of a stone wall. On the north, east, and south there is a ditch, beyond which is a surrounding bailey with its own ditch, crossed by a causeway on the south. The site is now rather obscured by modern forestry. This castle was probably built in the late 11th century. It was in royal hands from 1155 until restored to the de Lacys c1217. The £600 which Gilbert de Lady borrowed from Water de Lacy of Weobley in 1244 may have been for the building of walls here.

CHANSTONE TUMP   SO 366359

SE of Vowchurch church is an oval mound 4m high with a ditch which was filled by the adjacent River Dore. There are signs of possible stonework and there may have been a bailey on the north side. William Devereux held the manor from Walter de Lacy at the time of Domesday and his descendants were still there in 1243. There is a second mound at SO 367358 on the other side of the River Dore.

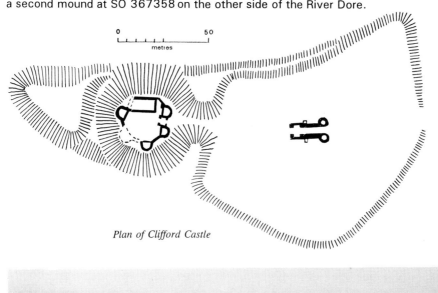

Plan of Clifford Castle

Chanstone Motte

The hall block at Clifford

CLIFFORD CASTLE   SO 243457

This castle was founded by William Fitz-Osbern in 1069-70 and was accompanied by a settlement which had 16 burgesses at the time of Domesday Book in 1086. By that time it had been granted to Ralph de Tosny. His daughter Margaret married Richard Fitz-Pons and their son Walter took the surname de Clifford. His daughter was "the fair Rosamund", the celebrated mistress of Henry II. It was probably the third Walter de Clifford, who succeeded in 1221, who built the small stone court with a hall and five D-shaped towers on the motte. The buildings were probably complete by 1233 when Henry II ordered Walter to pay off the large debts that he owed to the Jews, probably a result of the expense of the new works. Walter made the royal messenger "eate the King's Writ, Waxe and all" and the incensed king besieged and captured the castle in August of that year. On Walter's death in 1263 Clifford passed to Matilda Clifford, widow of William Longspey, Earl of Salisbury. She was abducted and forcibly married to John Giffard of Brimpsfield who was subsequently fined for this exploit, although the couple stayed together. Robert Clifford, great grandson of Walter III's cousin Roger, was created Lord of Westmorland in 1310 and from then until the line became extinct in 1675 the chief family seat was at Skipton in Yorkshire, where the castle has a remarkably similar plan form to Clifford.

The daughter of Matilda Clifford and John Giffard married Henry de Lacy, Earl of Lincoln, on whose death in 1311 Clifford passed to the Mortimers of Wigmore. They entertained Richard II and John of Gaunt at Clifford Castle in 1381 and garrisoned it against the Welsh in 1403. However Sir Edmund Mortimer was then Owain Glyndwr's prisoner at Harlech and forced to change sides, resulting in Clifford and Glasbury being given by Henry IV in 1404 to Sir Robert Witney in gratitude for the services of his father as sheriff of Herefordshire during this time of unrest. The castle was subsequently little used and fell into decay. In 1547 Clifford was granted to Lord Clinton but his heirs appear to have sold it not long afterwards. It was later held by the Wardour family.

The castle consists of a large mound rising 26m above the south bank of the River Wye, with a small triangular bailey, now very overgrown, to the west, and a much larger, lower and less well-defended enclosure to the east. The west bailey shows no sign of stone buildings. A mound in the middle of the east bailey was excavated in 1951-4 by Air Commodore Douglas Iron and found to contain the lower portion of a substantial gatehouse 8m wide by 16m long with turrets 5.7m in diameter projecting from the eastern corners. The turrets were solid at ground level but contained tiny circular rooms higher up. The passage was closed by a portcullis halfway along its length and has two recesses in the side walls of the inner section. Short stubs of curtain walling 2m thick adjoin the side walls but there are no other remains of the bailey wall. It was either never completed or was thoroughly destroyed. In 1657 the chancel of the castle chapel was still standing in the eastern, unwalled, part of the bailey. The house on the site may incorporate some of its materials.

On the mound summit are ruins of a D-shaped polygonal enclosure measuring about 20m across within a wall 2m thick, the longest side facing north towards the river and having a block 5.4m wide and 12.5m long abutting against it. This contained a hall over two dark storerooms. The hall has window embrasures in the north wall and there were probably others on the south side, which is missing at the upper level. On the east side of the court is a gateway passage with a portcullis groove flanked by D-shaped towers about 7.5m in diameter over walls 2m thick These towers are reduced to about 1m high, as is another tower facing south, whilst very little remains of a SW tower, but a west-facing tower still stands two storeys high. It had three arrow loops at court level and there were windows both towards the court and the field for the room above, which has a passage to a pair of latrines in the curtain wall thickness to the south. There are no signs of other chambers within the court so the hall block plus two rooms in each of the five towers, plus other rooms over the gateway and between it and the hall evidently formed enough accommodation.

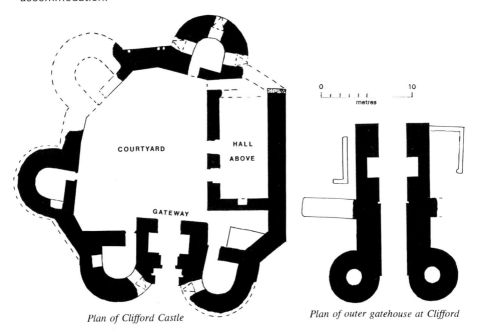

Plan of Clifford Castle

Plan of outer gatehouse at Clifford

Inner gatehouse tower at Clifford

COMBE MOTTE   SO 348635

The small mound 2.5m high near the confluence of the Hindwell Brook with the River Lugg has traces of a bailey to the east. Flooding has caused silting up of the ditches. John de la Combe witnessed charters of 1244 and 1249 concerning Presteigne.

Outer gatehouse at Clifford

Croft Castle

CROFT CASTLE   SO 449655   O

Domesday Book records Bernard de Croft as holding Croft, Wharton and Newton from William de Scholes. The Crofts appear to have had a residence on this site throughout the medieval period and parts of the outer walls and the four round corner towers of the existing building go back to the late 14th century or early 15th century. Leland records the house as being "sett on the browe of a hill, somewhat rokky, dychid and waulled castle-like". The Crofts were almost continuously represented in Parliament from 1296 until 1727 and were often sheriffs of Herefordshire. They were closely linked with the Mortimers of Wigmore. Sir Richard Croft held important positions in Edward IV's household and under Henry VII became Treasurer, a Privy Councillor and Steward to Prince Arthur at Ludlow. Although temporarily in disgrace during Queen Mary's reign, his great-grandson Sir James, who died in 1590, held various appointments under Edward VI and Elizabeth I.It was he who rebuilt the north side of the house and planted the avenues of oak and chestnut trees in the grounds. his grandson Sir Herbert Croft and his kinsmen the Scudamores, the Wigmores and the Warnecombes had a feud with Thomas Coningsby of Hampton Court which amounted to almost a private war. Subsequently he embraced the Catholic faith and died in 1629 as a monk at Douai in Flanders.

Sir Herbert's son Sir William was a Royalist who fared badly in the Civil War. According to a Parliamentary news sheet Croft Castle was plundered by Irish levies to whom the Royalists owed pay, and shortly afterwards the castle was dismantled to prevent it being occupied by Parliamentary troops, whilst Sir William was killed close to the castle in June 1645 after being pursued following skirmish at Stokesay. In 1671 Sir Herbert Croft, son of Dr Herbert Croft, Bishop of Hereford, was made a baronet by Charles II. His son Sir Arthur got into debt and the castle was transferred to Richard Knight of Downton in 1746. His son-in-law Thomas Johnes built the present entrance in the east range, probably on the site of a gatehouse demolished during the Civil War. The second Thomas Jones disposed of Croft to Somerset Davies of Wigmore, who was living in the castle in 1785. In 1923 his descendants, the Kevill-Davies, sold the castle to the Trustees of Sir James Croft, 11th baronet, then a minor. The Crofts still live in the castle, although the buildings and grounds are now maintained by the National Trust.

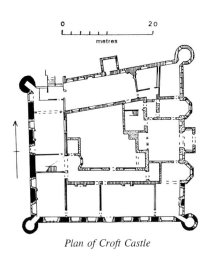

Plan of Croft Castle

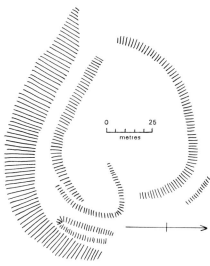

Plan of Cusop Castle

The medieval castle measured 30m from east to west within walls up to 1.2m thick. The south corners are right-angles but the east wall extends further north than the west wall. At each corner is a round tower 3.3m in diameter containing tiny rooms. It is likely that the central courtyard was originally reached through a gatehouse on the east side and that the medieval hall was in the west range, whilst there were two storey ranges on the north and south sides of the court. No medieval features now remain in any of the four ranges around the courtyard, all of which are now of three storeys, with a consequent heightening of the outer walls and towers in the 16th century. The corbelling on the towers marks the base of the original parapets. The 16th century north range now contains a kitchen and library. The east range is of c1750-60, and the porch and existing parapet and gables on the south front are of 1913. There are numerous Elizabethan and Georgian windows. The west wing was continued northwards by a 17th century extension demolished in 1937. The moat was probably filled in during or after the Civil War.

CUBLINGTON CASTLE   SO 406384

The badly damaged mound at Castle Farm (which has a 17th century house) is probably the site of the castle of the Delafield family. A bailey platform to the east has traces of a ditch on the west and south once filled by a stream. Between here and Madley parish church is a small overgrown moated site.

CUSOP CASTLE   SO 239414

SW of the church is a large enclosure with steep natural slopes to the SW and south. A road has replaced a ditch on the north and NW. Traces of footings of a curtain wall and buildings on the south side have been noted, and the base of a stone gateway was said to have been seen in the late 18th century. Cusop belonged to the Clavenogh family but was held by Henry ap Gruffydd in the early 14th century.

DILWYN CASTLE   SO 416544

On the south side of the village is a moated platform about 50m across with traces of buried footings of a curtain wall. An excavation revealed a corner of a square building with walling 2m thick thought to have been a keep. On the east was an outer bailey, also wet moated. During the 12th century Dilwyn was the seat of the descendants of Godfrey de Gamages, but by the early 13th century was held by William de Braose. The manor was later split into two parts held by the Fitz Warines and the Mallorys, one of which probably created the square moated site at SO 418538 1km south of the church with remains of a bridge abutment. A second possible early castle site lies west of this moat at SO 416538, whilst south of Little Dilwyn Farm at SO 438539 is another moated platform and probable deserted village.

DORSTONE CASTLE   SO 312417

West of the village is a mound rising 9m to a flat summit 33m by 26m on which was a shell keep. Excavation revealed a postern doorway in the side of a D-shaped tower flanking an entrance with a portcullis groove, and the bases of what were thought to be buttresses. There are buried foundations in the bailey to the east which was protected by a stream on the north side. The ditch on the east now lies under gardens. The earthworks may go back to about the time of Domesday Book, when "Dodintune" was held by Drogo Fitz Poyntz. The castle was held by the de Sollers family from the late 12th century until the 14th century. It was granted to Sir Walter Fitzwalter by Henry IV in 1403 and was then probably refortified. It may well have been destroyed by Owain Glyndwr soon afterwards for it is not mentioned again.

DOWNTON-ON-THE-ROCK CASTLE   SO 427735

The 3m high mound has a depression on top with stone debris and appears to be the remains of an octagonal or circular tower with a forebuilding on one side. There are traces of a bailey and other enclosures, now much altered.

0   metres   50

Eardisland Castle

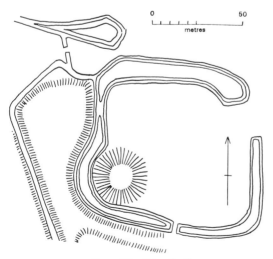

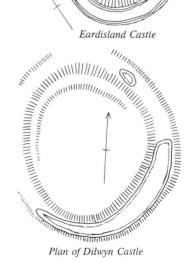

Plan of Eardisley Castle

Plan of Dilwyn Castle

EARDISLAND CASTLE   SO 421586

North of the church is a tree-clad mound with a summit 22m across rising 5m above a wet moat once crossed by a causeway on the NW side. The moat is fed by a channel from the River Arrow about 90m to the north. The stream on the east and the lane to the church on the west and SW probably mark the site of the bailey. Eardisland was held by the Pembridge family under the de Braoses and later was held by the Twyfords. At Monk's Court on the other side of the river at SO 420588 is a ditched mound 1.5m high, whilst 14th century Burton Court at SO 423573 lies in the assumed bailey of a mutilated motte.

EARDISLEY CASTLE   SO 311491

The rectangular moated enclosure measuring about 95m by 75m with a mound in the SW corner is assumed to be the site of Roger de Lacy's "domus defensibilis" mentioned in Domesday Book in 1086. The mound rises 4m above the bailey to a top 13m across and could be the buried base of a 13th century circular tower keep. There are signs of wall footings leading from it to the base of a D-shaped tower on the south side of the bailey. On the north side are two lengths of medieval battered walls incorporated in 17th and 18th century farm buildings. To the west are a pair of outer enclosures with wet moats fed by a stream, and traces have been located of what was interpreted as an outer gatehouse with a drawbridge pit. The de Bohun Earls of Hereford were later overlords of Eardisley until their male line died out in 1372 but the castle was occupied by tenants. In 1263 Roger de Clifford was in possession and it was here that he imprisoned the unpopular foreign Bishop of Hereford, Peter de Aquablanca. In 1272 William Baskerville was licensed to hold services in the chapel of the castle and their chief seat lay here until their fortunes declined in the early 17th century. The castle was said to be ruinous in 1374 but in 1403 it was refortified by Nicholas Montgomery against Owain Glyndwr on the orders of Henry IV. Most of the buildings were demolished during the Civil War although the last Baskerville occupied the gatehouse in a state of poverty until 1670, when the estate passed to William Barnesley. The existing farmhouse in the bailey dates from the 18th century.

EATON CAMP   SO 455394

At the east corner of the former Iron Age camp is what looks like a motte with traces of stonework on the adjoining ramparts.

EATON TREGOZ CASTLE   SO 605281 or 612287

Nothing now remains of the seat of the Tregoz family in the 12th and 13th centuries. The castle chapel is mentioned in 1280. On the death of John Tregoz in 1302 the castle passed to William de Grandison, who in 1309 was licensed to crenellate it. In 1375 the castle passed to the Watertons. When it passed in 1420 to the Abrahall family, who remained in possession until 1673, the castle had a hall with a buttery and pantry and a great chamber above, a parlour, a chapel, several other chambers, a kitchen, a bakehouse and brewery, stables and barns, two gateways with chambers above them and two mills. The site was either at Camp Field where there are traces of a mound and bailey with indications of former stonework, or, more likely, at Court Farm, where there is a vaulted cellar with an ogee-arched doorway and in the 1970s dressed stones from medieval windows were visible.

ECCLESWALL CASTLE   SO 652232

East of Eccleswall Court are slight remains of the Talbots' original Herefordshire seat until they obtained Goodrich Castle in 1326. The platform has traces of a ditch on the south and a retaining wall rising from a pool on the north, where there is a terrace to the east. The farm buildings contain re-used material and include an old dovecote.

EDVIN LOACH CASTLE   SO 662584

A ruined 11th century church lies inside the bailey, the ditch of which has been filled in during works associated with adapting the Victorian church on the edge of the motte ditch into a private residence.

EDVIN RALPH CASTLE   SO 644575

A low moated platform 37m across 100m west of the church has traces of a curtain wall and signs of a possible gatehouse towards a bailey on the north side which may also have been stone walled.

ELLINGHAM CASTLE   SO 662333

The 16th and 17th century house called Hellens NE of Much Marcle appears to be on or near the site of a castle of the Helyon family, who were tenants of the de Audleys. The name Quarry Wood given the site by Blount in the 17th century suggests it was then being plundered for building materials.

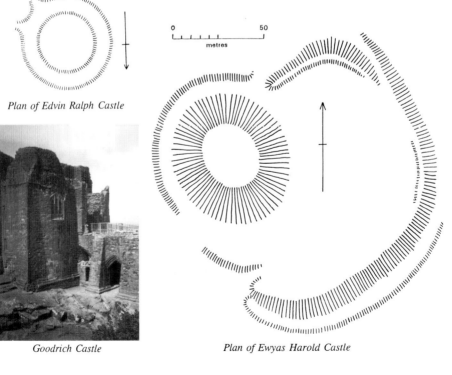

Plan of Edvin Ralph Castle

0   50
metres

Goodrich Castle

Plan of Ewyas Harold Castle

EWYAS HAROLD CASTLE   SO 384287   V

This is generally accepted as the site of a castle built c1050 by Osbern Pentecost. To it some of the Normans at King Edward the Confessor's court retreated when Earl Godwin returned from exile in 1052. It was refortified by William Fitz Osbern in 1067-71, having probably been slighted either by Earl Godwin or the Welsh, and at the time of Domesday Book was held by the original builder's nephew Alfred of Marlborough. The Harold part of the name refers to the son of Ralph of Mantes who was given the castle by William II in the 1090s. His son Robert moved the village out of the southern outer bailey of the castle and founded a Benedictine priory nearby. Ewyas Harold passed by marriage to Robert Tregoz in the 13th century and after John Tregoz died in 1302 it passed by marriage to Roger de la Warre. His grandson Sir Roger de la Warre took King John of France prisoner at Poitiers in 1356. The castle was given by Henry IV in 1403 to Sir Philip le Vache with the intention that it should be refortified against Owain Glyndwr, but later the same year custody of it was given to Sir William Beauchamp, Lord Bergavenny, from whose heirs it passed to the Nevilles. The castle played no further part in history, being ruined when Leland saw it c1540, and "ruynous and gone" in 1645.

The remains comprise a D-shaped bailey platform 110m in diameter with a large motte near the west end of the vulnerable straight NW side. The motte has been formed by cutting through the neck of a natural spur with a great ditch, and rises 13m above that ditch to a summit 32m across which is 15m above the bailey. Debris and quarry pits on the mound summit (which is less densely overgrown than the slopes) indicate the former presence of a shell keep with a wall said to have been 2.7m thick and flanked by D-shaped towers. It is uncertain whether the bailey was ever stone walled but it certainly contained a stone chapel of St Nicholas.

Site of stables, Goodrich

Goodrich: the gatehouse viewed from the keep

GILLOW MANOR   SO 532254

This is a 14th century mansion with four ranges around a tiny court entered through a projecting and embattled gatehouse with a vaulted passage on the SW side. The other ranges have been mostly rebuilt. A moat formerly surrounded the house and enclosed an outer court on the SW.

GOODRICH CASTLE   SO 577200   E

This castle takes its name from Godric Mapplestone, who held Hulle (or Howl) nearby at the time of Domesday. He is assumed to have founded a castle in the 1090s and it is mentioned as Godric's Castle in 1101, although it is possible that the site then occupied was Great Howle Camp at SO 611201, a rectangular ringwork with a rampart 3m high with traces of a ditch and evidence of burning, Saxo-Norma pottery having been found on the site. William Fitz Baderon, Lord of Monmouth held Goodrich in 1146, possibly having illegally seized it during the anarchy of Stephen's reign. The present castle existed by the 1160s, having a tower keep of that period, possibly built by Richard de Clare, the famous "Strongbow". Henry II's Pipe Rolls of 1178 note expenditure on the castle, which was then in his possession. In 1201 King John granted Goodrich to William Marshall, Earl of Pembroke, who had married Strongbow's heiress in 1189. He or one his five sons who each in turn succeeded him built a curtain wall with round corner towers. When Walter Marshalls died at Goodrich in 1245 the castle reverted to the Crown but in 1247 was granted by Henry III to his kinsman William de Valance, who had married Joan de Munchesney, a co-heiress of the Marshall estates. William is thought to have rebuilt the castle in the 1280s and used it as a convenient stopping place halfway between his English and Welsh estates.

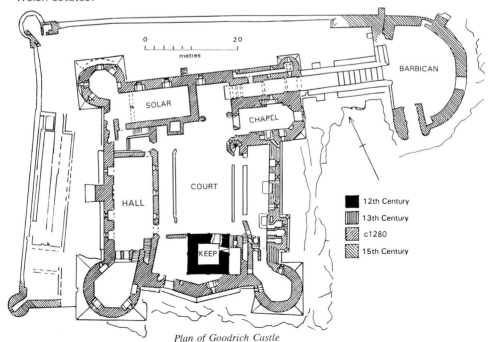

Plan of Goodrich Castle

Doorway in solar block at Goodrich

The gatehouse at Goodrich

When William's son Aymer died in 1324 Goodrich passed to his niece Elizabeth Comyn. She was abducted by the younger Hugh Despenser and forced to resign her rights to the estate to him. She later married Richard Talbot, and after the fall from power of Edward II and the hated Despensers in 1326 he seized the castle, which was subsequently confirmed to him and his wife by Edward III. The castle became the principal residence of their successors, who became earls of Shrewsbury in 1446. The Lancastrian 3rd Earl, John, was forfeited after Edward IV took the throne in 1461 and Goodrich was held by William Herbert until the earl was reconciled with the king and restored to his estates. The earls of Shrewsbury later developed other residences elsewhere and Goodrich was little used during the latter part of the 16th century. It was unoccupied in 1616, when the 7th Earl, Gilbert, died and the castle passed to his daughter Elizabeth and her husband Henry Grey, Earl of Kent.

In 1642 the castle was garrisoned for Parliament by Colonel Robert Kyrle but in December a large Royalist force from South Wales was able to take possession. As Parliament's strength grew during 1645 the garrison under Sir Henry Lingen found itself increasing isolated, although they were able to cause considerable disruption to local communications. A surprise attack succeeded in burning the stables in the outer ward and at the beginning of June 1646 Colonel John Birch began a regular siege. The mortar called Roaring Meg, now at Hereford, caused much damage to the castle, especially to the cisterns and the piped water supply from outside was cut off. The deep well in the courtyard was presumably by then not in use. Mining and countermining were employed but after part of the NW tower collapsed and blocked a countermine, leaving a breach, Lingen and his men surrendered on 31st July. The castle was ordered to be slighted in 1647 but seems to have been totally wrecked during the siege so that little was done beyond taking away lead from the remaining roofs. The Countess of Kent was offered £1,000 by Parliament in compensation. In 1740 the Earl of Kent sold Goodrich to Admiral Thomas Griffin. It then passed through various families until 1920 when it was placed in state care, custody now being in the hands of English Heritage.

Goodrich: The keep and SE tower

The form of the original castle is uncertain, the bare sandstone shelf commanded by higher ground on two sides being ill suited to defences of earth and timber, which rather begs the question of what accompanied the tower keep when it was built in the 1160s. This keep is the smallest of its type in England, having ashlar faced walls 2.2m thick with thin buttresses at the corners and in the middle of each side enclosing dark rooms 4.5m square. The keep is 16.5m high and contained a hall over a low cellar and a private room on top. The existing roof is flat but the original must have been gabled with the apex roughly at the height of the now-destroyed wall-walk. The original doorway, now converted into a window, is at hall level and has one order of shafts. Until a doorway was later broken through at ground level the basement can only have been reached by a trap-door and ladder from above. It is lighted by a single loop. From the hall a spiral stair in the NW corner rises to the upper levels. A string course with chevron ornamentation marks the top storey, which has two-light round-arched windows to the west and north.

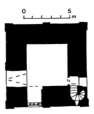

Keep plan, Goodrich

Goodrich: the NW tower from the keep

All that remains of the early 13th century rebuilding of the castle are parts of the east curtain wall, the footings of a round Sw tower within the much larger tower now there, and the reset piscina of the chapel. The rest of the castle was rebuilt in the 1280s, Edward I aiding the work by having oaks sent from the Forest of Dean. Walls about 2.5m thick were built around a rectangular court with ranges of apartments on each side, a gatehouse at the NE corner, and large round towers rising from square bases with distinctive tall pyramidal spurs at the other three corners.

The gateway is approached by a ramp which formerly had a drawbridge at the inner end. The passageway was closed by at least two sets of doors and two portcullises, and there is a machicolation from the room above. On the north side of the passage is a mural corridor to a latrine and a small porter's room formed in the base of a round turret, whilst on the south side is a chapel with a polygonal apse set within a rounded outer section. The large mullioned window in the apse is a 16th century insertion. Adjoining the chapel is a polygonal stair turret leading to a fine suite of upper chambers for the use of the constable.

The gateway passage opens into a square space later enclosed to carry additional rooms above. This leads into the north end of a rectangular court, along the east and west sides of which were formerly low lean-to roofed corridors as in a monastic cloister. The east range was probably used by retainers and had another storey added to it later. A projection from the east wall contains a complex series of latrines. The hall occupies the west range with an ante-room between it and the solar in the north range. The solar west end was divided off by a pair of arches on a pier continued down through a servant's hall underneath, below courtyard level. Bedrooms were provided in the NW tower. which is now very ruined, and a small chapel lay over the ante-room. In the 15th century the solar was heightened and an intermediate floor inserted to create more chambers. A gallery was then provided to link the upper rooms with an upper gallery in the west end of the chapel, where a doorway now lies isolated high up. In the thick outer walls the hall and solar have long single-light windows with transoms and seats in the embrasures, and the hall has remains of a fine fireplace. The keep occupies the middle part of the south range with the curtain projected out as a spur behind it. To the east is a vaulted strongroom or prison, and to the west is a kitchen with several ovens. Beyond these are long flights of steps to the uppermost rooms in the southern towers. These were large and pleasant rooms with fine fireplaces intended for important officials or guests.

Goodrich Castle from across the River Wye

The castle walls were built from material taken from the deep and wide rock-cut ditch isolating the sandstone platform from the rest of the ridge to the south and east. On the other sides is a level shelf forming an outer ward enclosed by a thin wall with round turrets on the west corners. The walls and the timber-framed stables within them are mostly reduced to footings. Beyond the ground falls away steeply to the River Wye on the north and to a tributary brook on the west. On the east side, beyond the ramp to the gatehouse is a semi-circular barbican with thick walls and its own narrow rock-cut ditch. Like the outer court this may be as late as c1310-20, although copied from a similar barbican built at the Tower of London in 1279. From it there was access to the stables in the outer ward.

GREAT HOWLE CAMP   SO 611201

This is a rectangular enclosure with round corners and a rampart 3m high with a ditch. Saxo-Norman pottery has been found here together with evidence of burning.

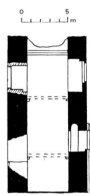

Gatehouse machicolations, Hampton Court

Keep section, Goodrich

Hampton Court

Plan of Hampton Court

Gateway, Hampton Court

HAMPTON COURT   SO 515527

The de Hamptons had a manor house here in the 13th century but the present mansion was built by Sir Rowland Lenthall from the proceeds of the ransoms of French nobles captured at the battle of Agincourt in 1415. The original crenellations, long since rebuilt, were licensed by Henry VI in 1434. Leland says that Rowland ceased building operations after the death of his only son but there is nothing in the structure to confirm this. Rowland's daughter married Thomas Cornwall, whose grandson sold the mansion c1510 to Sir Humphrey Coningsby. His descendant Thomas was created Lord Coningsby by William III as a reward for saving the king's life the day before his victory over the Catholic army of James II at the battle of the Boyne in Ireland in 1689. Early 18th century Lord Coningsby commissioned Colin Campbell to rebuild the house. He became Lord Lieutenant of Herefordshire in 1715 but was a noted tyrant and by the 1720s was a prisoner in the Tower of London, having libelled Lord Macclesfield, the Chancellor. Further remodelling was undertaken in the 1790s for Thomas's great-grandson George, 5th Earl of Essex, but the house was sold to Richard Arkwright in 1808 and his grandson John carried out more work on it in the 1830s. The Arkwrights sold the court in 1912 and in 1924 it was acquired by Viscountess Hereford, whose family held it until the 1970s. It has recently been sold to an American firm for conversion to a conference centre.

The house has four irregular ranges set around a rectangular central court. Much of the building now dates from the 18th and 19th centuries and the chief medieval survivals are the substantial gatehouse on the north with a portcullis groove in the outer portal, the lower parts of the north ranges with small rectangular turrets at the ends, the chapel which projects eastward from the north end of the east front, and the porch in the middle of the north side of the south range, which originally led into the screens passage at the west end of the hall. All the windows in these parts are later replacements. The upper part of the north front has rainwater heads dated 1710 with the arms of the first Lord Coningsby and his second wife Frances Jones.

HEREFORD CASTLE   SO 512396   F

Ralph de Mantes, Earl of Hereford built a castle here c1050. It was destroyed in 1055, but was rebuilt, perhaps on a larger scale, by William Fitz-Osbern in 1067. The Saxon leader Edric the Wild made an unsuccessful attack upon it in that year. Geoffrey Talbot held Hereford against King Stephen, who besieged and captured the city and castle in 1138 after a siege lasting about a month, during which much of the city was burnt down. Geoffrey returned in 1140 with Miles of Gloucester and recaptured the castle after a vigorous siege in which it was bombarded with stones from a siege engine mounted on the cathedral tower and an unsuccessful attempt was made by Stephen to relieve it. Miles, who was created Earl of Hereford by the Empress Matilda in 1141, caused great offence when during his attempt to capture the motte during the siege he had a ditch and rampart cut through part of the cemetery of the collegiate church of St Guthlac, which lay in the castle bailey, and many buried bodies were revealed and left exposed.

On his accession in 1154 Henry II confirmed Miles' son Roger in possession of Hereford Castle, only to confiscate it when Roger rebelled in 1155. It then remained in royal hands, the houses on the motte (presumably still of wood), being repaired in 1165 and 1169. At some period between then and the 1240s they were replaced by a large stone keep. The castle was strengthened during the rebellion by the king's sons in 1173-4 and the bailey defences were at least partly of stone by 1181-2 when a defective section of walling was demolished and rebuilt. Further work was carried out during Prince John's revolt in 1191-3. John, as king, has a small tower built in 1202-3. Timber for hoarding was sent to the garrison in 1213, and the castle was fortified against the Welsh in 1215-6.

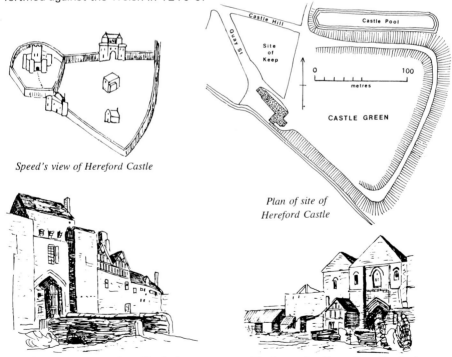

Speed's view of Hereford Castle

Plan of site of
Hereford Castle

The former Widemarsh Gate, Hereford

The former Bye Street Gate, Hereford

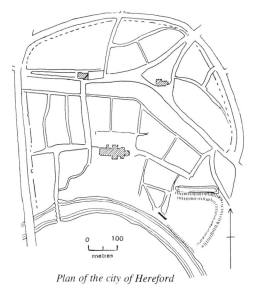

Plan of the city of Hereford

Water Gate, Hereford Castle

It was probably Henry III who surrounded the tower keep with a walled court with several towers. Leland says there were ten semi-circular towers and Speed's map of 1610 suggests that there were about six towers on the court around the keep and two towers at each of the main gate on the north side of the bailey and the postern gate facing the river at the SW corner of the bailey. He also shows St Guthlac's church, foundations of which were revealed by excavation in 1960. There is no specific mention of major new works in the royal accounts but continual repairs are noted, and a new tower was built in 1239-40 to replace one that had fallen. Despite over £100 being spent on the castle in 1250-2 a survey of 1254 reported that the keep roof needed repair and the steps up to it needed rebuilding, whilst the Jews' prison below the wall around the keep was roofless, the gatehouses needed repair and much of the wall facing the Wye on the SW side was being undermined by the river. A quay was subsequently built there to solve this problem.

Much is recorded of the domestic buildings at this time, all of which have now vanished. The bailey contained the king's great hall, the king's small hall, the county hall, private chambers for the king and queen and their knights, an almonry, a counting house or treasury, a stable, two gaols, a building which housed siege engines, and various offices and service rooms including a kitchen and bakery. In 1245 the king's chamber was whitewashed and wainscoted, whilst the queen's chamber was lengthened, wainscoted, painted and provided with a wardrobe, fireplace and latrine. A chapel built alongside the king's chamber in 1233 was already in need of repair in 1254. It was probably this chapel that was rebuilt in 1283-5. A new kitchen for the king's household was built in 1256, and in the 1260s a new chamber was built for the royal clerks.

Hereford supported Simon de Montfort against King Henry and withstood an attack by Roger Mortimer in 1264. De Montfort governed England from the city whilst King Henry and his son Edward, captured at the battle of Lewes, were kept prisoner in the castle. Edward was allowed to ride outside the walls and he escaped to the Mortimer stronghold of Wigmore after organising races to tire out his guards' mounts so that they were unable to pursue him.

Hereford Castle was little used after the defeat of the Welsh and surveys of 1291 and 1300 record several roofs as needing repair and that a section of the outer wall had collapsed. When Queen Isabella visited Hereford in 1326 she stayed in the Bishop's palace as the castle was then too neglected to accommodate her. It seems that some repairs were executed but it was not until 1402, during Owain Glyndwr's revolt against Henry IV, that further major repairs were undertaken. A long section of the river wall had collapsed and the breach was filled with a paling made from 351 oaks felled in Haywood Forest, whilst the keep was reroofed and other towers patched up. Leland c1540 described the castle as having been "one of the fairest, largest, and strongest castles in England", but comments that it was "tendeth toward ruin". He describes the "great bridge of stone arches, and a drawbridge in the middle of it", which formed the approach to the north gatehouse as "now clean down", and also mentions the spring which provided the water supply and the mill inside the bailey driven by a brook draining out of the moat.

The castle does not seem to have played an independent part during the sieges and occupations of the city in the Civil War and it merely formed part of the defensive circuit. It appears, however, to have suffered considerable damage at this time, and most of what remained was demolished in the mid 1650s to provide material for building a new dining hall for the college of the Vicars' Choral and other structures within the city. A map made in 1677 shows only the motte, the moats, the main gatehouse and the watergate. The motte was later entirely removed and also the main gatehouse, but the building remaining in the SW corner of the bailey appears to incorporate parts of the 13th century watergate, although no features of interest survive within it. The large bailey became a public park in the mid 18th century and the ramparts on the north and east sides appear to be at least partly of that era. The east moat is dry but the northern arm of the moat still retains over 20m width of water, quite a formidable barrier.

Excavations have revealed remains of a timber-revetted rampart and ditch erected around the city of Hereford in the 9th century. It appears to have enclosed an almost square area north of the Wye with the cathedral occupying the SW quarter and a cross-pattern of streets with main gates in the middle of each side. The defended area was later extended to the east to enclose the church of St Guthlac, and in the early 10th century the rampart was externally faced with stone, although probably still with a timber superstructure. The defences appear to have been in a neglected state in 1055 when the Welsh captured and sacked the city and burnt the cathedral.

Moat of Hereford Castle

City wall at Hereford

The charter granted to the city in 1189 and the threat of further Welsh attacks prompted considerable new work on the defences in the 1190s. Four new gatehouses, probably of timber, were built, and the enclosed area was extended to the north, whilst the Row Ditch south of the river may have been a work of this period to protect a suburb there. The town was held for Prince John in 1197 and had to be captured by the Justiciar Hubert Walter. Henry III, on a visit to Hereford in 1223, evidently regarded the defences as inadequate and he authorised the bailiffs to charge tolls on merchandise entering the city for the purpose of erecting a new stone wall. It was built in front of the older rampart and was up to 2m thick and 5.5m high with six stone gatehouses, 17 D-shaped towers, and a deep wet moat in front fed by the Yazor Brook. One gatehouse stood at the south end of the bridge over the Wye and others closed off St Nicholas Street (Friars' Gate), Eign Street, Widemarsh Street, Bye Street and St Owen's Street.

In spite of the cost of maintenance the city walls appear to have been kept in a reasonable condition throughout the later medieval period, and Leland found them in good order. By his time individual citizens were each expected to maintain a short section, called a loop. In 1596 a tower near St Owen's Gate was rented to William Wellington on condition that he kept it in repair. However it would appear that the walls needed considerable repairs to make them defensible in the Civil War. The city submitted to roving Parliamentary armies in October 1642 and April 1643 without resistance, but a Royalist garrison under Barnaby Scudamore made a much more determined defence against a Scottish army under the Earl of Leven in the summer of 1645. The circuit of the walls remained almost intact when Taylor's map was made in 1757, but the gateways were destroyed at the end of the 18th century, and subsequently much of the walls themselves were robbed for building materials.

The ring-road around the NE, north and west sides of the city centre lie on the site of the former moat. Sections of the north and NE parts of the wall are marked by thin walling of fairly recent date. Genuine original portions of the wall only remain on the west side of the city, a considerable section 2m high with one round tower remaining between the sites of the Eign Gate and Friars' Gate, whilst the next section reaching almost to the river is even better preserved. It has small pilaster buttresses suggesting a 12th century date for this part, and is nowhere more than 1m thick at present. It has one round 13th century tower 6m high with arrow loops high up.

Ringwork at the Herefordshire Beacon

HEREFORDSHIRE BEACON   SO 760401   F

An oval ringwork with a summit 50m long lies the highest central part of the Iron Age hillfort, which probably formed a bailey 130m by 100m surrounding it and having a ditch isolating it on the NE. Pottery found during an excavation in the 1870s was re-assessed in the 1950s as being 11th or 12th century. It has been suggested that the ringwork was erected by Harold Godwinson in c1055-65 since Norman castles were mostly low lying. In any case it is unlikely that this bare wind-swept hill 335m above sea-level and without a water supply was occupied for long.

HOW CAPLE MOTTE   SO 613306

A mound 3.5m high lies just SE of the church.

HUNTINGTON CASTLE   SO 249539   F

The remote parish of Huntington is enclosed by Wales on all sides except to the NE. The original castle of this district, founded either by Adam de Port c1070 or by Bernard de Newmarch in the 1090s was probably the motte known as Turret Castle on a spur in Hell Wood at SO 259534 1km east of the church. The mound rises 8m to a summit 23m across with traces of a shell keep and has a large bailey to the NE with traces of a curtain wall 1.6m thick. Foundations of a gatehouse can be traced on the east, where there was perhaps a second bailey. Another motte lies just south of Turret Castle at SO 258532, and to the SW at Little Hengoed is a 5m high mound at SO 246521 which possibly bore a stone tower, whilst yet another mound 3m high lies 0.5km beyond at SO 248516.

The castle site now known as Huntington 0.5km north of the parish church seems to have been established later on by the de Braose family, either during Stephen's reign, or possibly as late as the 1220s when it is first mentioned and replaced the castle of Kington as the seat of the barony of that name. Although it looks like a motte and bailey site of 12th century type much of the 9m high mound may in fact be mostly a stump of a round tower keep of c1220-40 buried in its own debris. This site overlooks a tributary of the Gladestry Brook and has an oval bailey 75m long by 60m wide with a 6m high fragment of a curtain wall remaining on the west and a fragment containing a stair of a D-shaped tower on the north, east of which is a causeway over the surrounding ditch. There are also slight traces of a D-shaped tower on the south. In recent years much of the undergrowth has been removed from the bailey. To the NE is a larger outer bailey defended by a ditch.

In 1248 Huntington passed to the de Bohun Earl of Hereford, and they were given permission in 1256 to hold a fair in the borough, the abandoned site of which lies to the south. In 1265 the castle was captured by Prince Edward from Earl Humphrey. The male line of the de Bohuns failed in 1372 and the heiress married Henry, Earl of Derby, son of John of Gaunt. When he took the throne in 1399 as Henry IV the earldom of Hereford passed to Edward Stafford, Earl of Buckingham. He was killed fighting for Henry IV at the battle of Shrewsbury in 1403 and his widow Anne later that year fortified the castle against Owain Glyndwr. The keep was then re-roofed, the main gate and postern gate rehung on fresh hinges and a new outer ditch and palisade constructed. The Staffords had little subsequent use for this remote stronghold and it was said to be so decayed that it was worthless in 1460. When the Stafford estates were surveyed after the forfeiture and execution of the Duke of Buckingham by Henry VIII in 1521 one tower remained in use as a prison. In 1564 Elizabeth I gave the manor to Sir Ambrose Cave, who later sold it to Sir Francis Vaughan. The estate subsequently passed through the Garner, Townsend, Holman, and Cheese families. Much of the walls still remained standing in 1670.

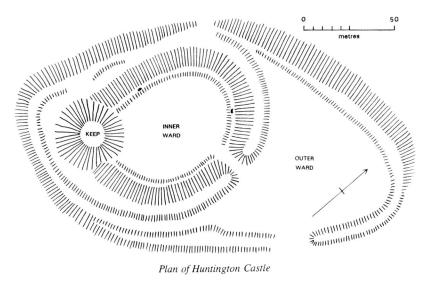

0   50
metres

KEEP

INNER WARD

OUTER WARD

Plan of Huntington Castle

HYDE CASTLE   SO 456553   V

A small part of the moat remains of a castle consisting of a low motte with a baileys to the south and a larger outer bailey to the west. There seems to have been a shell keep on the motte with a barbican on one side. A barn lies on the ditch of the southern bailey. Not far to the west is a platform with a silted-up moat and there is a circular moated platform with remains of a stone-faced dam at Upper Wintercott at SO 472547, 1.5km to the ESE.

KENDERCHURCH MOTTE   SO 415294

NE of Howton Farm between the A465 and the railway, 1.6km NE of the parish church, is a mound about 2m high with traces of a former ditch.

KENTCHURCH COURT   SO 421270

Kentchurch was long held by the Scudamores, who gradually altered a 14th century embattled mansion hidden away in a side valley into a comfortable country house. Here they may have sheltered their kinsman Owain Glyndwr for many years disguised as their parish priest. The rectangular NW tower perhaps originally functioned as a tower house. It was heightened in 1800 during alterations supervised by John Nash and was then given mullioned windows in each of the four storeys above the basement. A latrine projects from the NE corner at third storey level. The medieval hall lay in the east range. A range south of it was remodelled c1700 and again by Nash a century later. Original 14th century work survives also in the NE range and the SE gateway.

The mound rising 3m to a summit 16m by 13m in Bowlstone Court Wood on the hillside at SO 421270 1.3km to the north of the church, and the rectangular moated site east of the church at SO 421257 may mark earlier manorial seats, whilst the house at Twyn-y-Corras at SO 418249 lies in the bailey of a motte damaged by a former World War II pill box being built into it. Excavation in 1988 revealed footings of a Norman chapel in a second bailey to the east. The chapel had an apsidal east end, later squared off, and it was given a tower later on but was demolished c1400.

Kentchurch Court

0 ___ 5
metres

Kentchurch Court

Huntington Castle

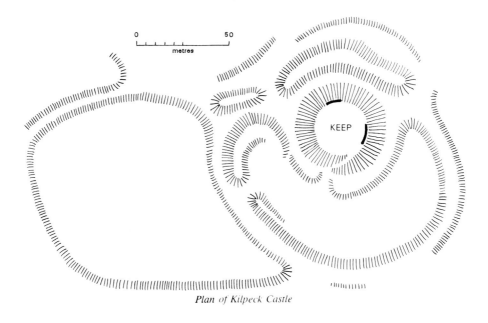

Plan of Kilpeck Castle

Kilpeck Castle

KILPECK CASTLE   SO 444305   F

William Fitz-Norman de Plies is assumed to have built this castle c1090 as the administrative centre of the ancient district of Archenfield. His grandson Henry took the surname de Kilpeck and Henry's son John purchased the barony of Pulverbatch in Shropshire in 1193. The chapel in the castle is mentioned in 1134, when its revenues were given to the newly founded priory along with those of the parish church. The castle is mentioned in the Pipe Rolls for 1189 and King John was entertained within in 1211, 1212, and 1214, his host being William de Cantilupe, Sheriff of Herefordshire, who had custody of John's young son's Hugh during his minority. It is presumed that by then the buildings on the mound had been rebuilt in stone. On the death of Hugh in 1244 the castle passed to his daughter Isabella, who married William Waleraund. In 1259 Henry III granted them permission to hold a weekly market and an annual fair at Kilpeck. On William's death in 1273 Kilpeck passed to Alan Plukenet. When his son Alan died in 1325 Kilpeck went to Eleanor de Bohun, who was married to James Butler, Earl of Ormond. With its lords living outside the country the castle rapidly fell into decay, as did the settlement outside its gates, the value of which had dropped by about two thirds when James died in 1338. Leland noted the "castel of Kilpeck by Herchenfeld belongging to the Erle of Ormond" or which "sum ruines of the waulles yet stonde". The decayed castle was nonetheless garrisoned by Royalists during the Civil War and was subsequently slighted by order of Parliament. The owners were then the Pyes of The Mynde.

The castle earthworks lie between the small but splendidly ornate church of c1140 to the east and a hollow to the west. They consists of a motte rising about 6m to a summit 28m in diameter with a large kidney-shaped bailey to the east with the graveyard now encroaching upon it and an outer bailey roughly 100m square to the south. There is an outer bank to the motte ditch on the west, where there is another outer bailey, whilst other outworks lay to the north and the medieval village was beyond the church. On the motte summit are two fragments of a shell keep wall about 2m thick and 5m high. Both have remains of round-backed fireplace flues of former internal lean-to buildings. The bailey seems to have had a stone gatehouse on the east side and there are indications of a former curtain wall. Nothing now survives of a 2m high mound at Digget's Wood, 1km to the SSW at SO 441295

KINGS CAPEL TUMP   SO 559288   V

The churchyard may represent the bailey of a 4m high mound to the SW with traces of the footings of a shell keep on the 23m diameter summit.

KINGSLAND CASTLE   SO 445613   V

On level ground west of the church is a 5m high mound with an oval summit 26m across. According to Leland part of a long abandoned keep (presumably a shell wall) was still standing on the summit in the 1530s. Two bailey platforms with modest ditches lie to the NE and SE and there are traces of a possible former village enclosure. The adjacent stream probably originally fed a series of wet moats. Henry I gave the former royal estate of Kingsland (hence the name) to Philip de Braose in the 1130s and the castle was probably founded about that time. King John stayed in the castle in 1216 whilst waging war on the forfeited de Braoses but it was probably abandoned during the 13th century.

KINGS PYON MOTTE   SO 442489

NE of the early 17th century Butthouse is a mound which rises 3m to a summit 16m across. There are also traces of a bailey with ploughed-out ditches.

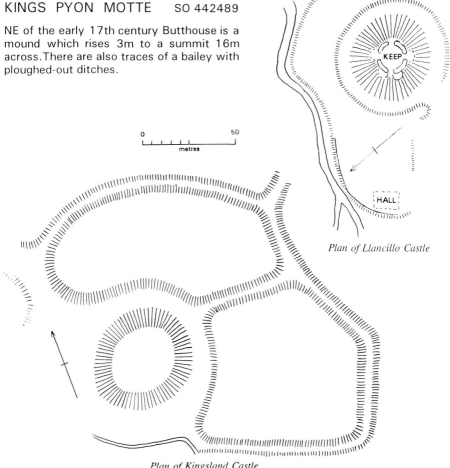

Plan of Llancillo Castle

Plan of Kingsland Castle

Kingsland Castle

KINGTON CASTLE   SO 292569

The field called Castle Hill north of the church and overlooking the Bach Brook is assumed to be the site of a castle built in the late 11th century as the seat of the barony of Kington. The palisade was repaired at the expense of Henry II in 1187. The castle is thought to have been destroyed by King John in August 1216 and the castle at Huntington then became the seat of the barony.

At Castle Twts 2km to the west at SO 277555 the base of a stone keep and bailey have been reported on a small knoll, although no stonework is currently visible. Nearby is the Vaughan seat of Hergest Court (SO 275553 which seems to have been protected by channelling water from the adjacent River Arrow. An outbuilding on the south may be 14th century but the main house is of c1430 and is of stone with some timber-framed parts. There is a low mound on which traces of a wall 12.5m thick have been noted at Woodville, 2.5km SE of Kington, at SO 304544. The mound seems to have once had a water-filled ditch. There is a possible motte and bailey site at Chickward, 3km SSW of Kington, at SO 287535. The mound is partly wet moated.

KINNERSLEY CASTLE   SO 346497

The Kinnersley family had a moated manor house here which passed to Richard de la Bere c1340. Buried footing probably survive and the and slight traces of the moat were visible on the north and east sides in the 1930s. It is thought there was a drawbridge on the east. The present L-plan house of three storeys above cellars below ground was built by Roger Vaughan c1585-90 and passed to Francis Smallman in 1633.

KINTON MOTTE   SO 408745

A house lies upon a mound 2.5m high 0.4km NE of Leintwardine church. One side has been cut away to make space for a previous house. The manor of Kinton was held at the time of Domesday by Richard de la Barre from Ralph de Mortimer.

LEMORE MOTTE   SO 310517

North of the farm is a circular platform with a partly water-filled moat. Traces of a wall 2m thick have been noted which is thought to have been a shell keep rising directly from the moat. There are also traces of a bailey, possibly also stone walled. Pottery of the 12th to the 14th centuries has been found on this site. At The Camp 2.4m to the west at SO 287520 is a circular enclosure 40m across with a dry ditch.

LEYSTERS MOTTE   SO 568632

South of the church is a mound rising 3m to a summit 23m in diameter. There are indications of a bailey to the south and a possible deserted village to the east.

LINGEN CASTLE   SO 366673

Immediately north of the church is a rectangular bailey platform 90m by 60m with a pond in the middle. At the east end a mound rises 6.5m above its ditch to a summit 18m across. There are indications the motte may have borne a shell keep, and the bailey was defended by a curtain wall and a water filled ditch fed by a stream. In 1086 Lingen was held by Thurston the Fleming from Ralph de Mortimer. Descended from him was the John de Lingen who in 1243 held a third of a knight's fee here from the lord of Wigmore. A ringwork about 35m across with traces of a bailey to the SE lies 1km to the NE at SO 372681.

LITTLE HEREFORD CASTLE   SO 555679

Around the church are various earthworks probably representing a small motte and bailey with a deserted village site, once the seat of the de la Mere family. Here King Stephen may have camped in 1140.

Gatehouse at Longtown

LLANCILLO CASTLE   SO 367256

The mound rises 8m to a summit 16m across with traces of what appears to be a crudely built shell keep with a gatehouse with twin round turrets facing towards a bailey with the buried stump of a hall block at the far end 35m away and what may be a D-shaped tower on the edge of the motte ditch. This castle is thought to have been built in the 1090s by Richard Esketot, a tenant of the de Lacys of Longtown. After the last of this line the castle was neglected by the absentee Aylesfords.

LONGTOWN CASTLE   SO 321292   F

This castle was probably built by Hugh de Lacy in the 1140s or 50s and is likely to be the new castle mentioned in the Pipe Rolls for 1187. £37 was then spent upon it and the older castle of Ewyas Lacy, which is assumed to be the 10m high motte with a crescent shaped bailey to the NE at Pont Hendre above the Olchon Brook at SO 326281, and which was captured by the Welsh in 1146. Hugh's son Walter, who inherited in 1189, is thought to have erected the stone keep and bailey curtain during the period 1216-31, when he was sheriff of Herefordshire. Henry III was at Longtown in 1233 and in the following year the castle was acquired by John Fitz-Geoffrey when he married the widow of Walter de Lacy's only son Gilbert. The castle later passed to Walter's daughter Margaret, who married John de Verdon. When their grandson Theobald died in 1316 Longtown passed by marriage to Bartholomew de Berghersh. His son Bartholomew died in 1369 and the castle then passed by marriage to the Despencers and then to the Beauchamps and the Nevilles. After 1316 the lords were absentees who allowed the castle to decay, although in 1403 Henry IV ordered it refortified against Owain Glyndwr. The cannon balls reputedly found near the keep may be evidence of an unrecorded action during the Civil War, but the castle was probably completely ruined by then.

Keep at Longtown

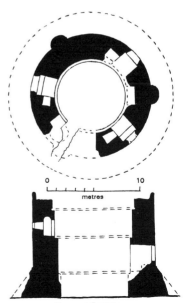

Keep at Longtown

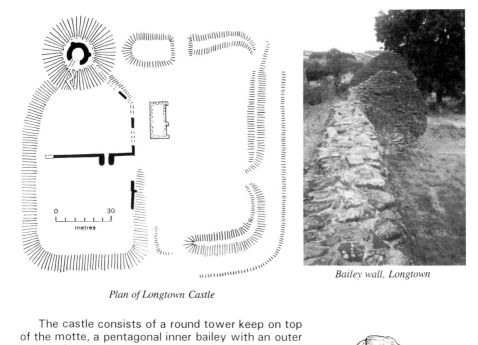

Bailey wall, Longtown

Plan of Longtown Castle

The castle consists of a round tower keep on top of the motte, a pentagonal inner bailey with an outer bailey about 46m square beyond it, and a larger eastern bailey beyond the modern road and enclosed by a high rampart once though to be of Roman origin. Dividing the two western baileys is a wall 1.8m thick now about 4m high. A gateway passage 1.8m wide with grooves for a portcullis lies near the east end. The 3m thick walls flanking the passage have rounded outer ends and thus formed solid turrets. Only fragments remain of the east and NE walls of the inner bailey and nothing at all of the west and NW sides, where there is now a hedge overlooking a steep slope. Of the southern bailey wall there are foundations on the south and a fragment on the east beside remains of a much later building.

Keep at Longtown

The keep measures 13.3m in diameter above a high and deeply battered plinth, the outer part of which is now broken away. Spaced evenly around the exterior were three semi-circular buttresses. One, now destroyed, strengthened the wall behind a spiral stair and had the entrance next to it, another contains a latrine opening off the topmost room, whilst the third backs onto a fireplace in the hall. This keep was once thought to contain just a hall with a dark bedroom above but such a layout would be very unusual and clearance in the 1970s revealed the expected basement, a low, featureless room that can only have been reached by a trap-door in the hall floor. The hall has three windows which were once of two narrow square-headed lights under a round outer arch. That facing NE has a reset stone with rosettes on the outer face. The embrasures each have a locker in one jamb. The two top storey windows are mere narrow loops. Above was a high conical roof with its timbers rising from an internal offset 1.2m below the wall-walk.

LOWER BROCKHAMPTON   SO 688560   O

A ruined Norman chapel lies beside a moated platform on which is a timber-framed hall probably built by John Domulton, who inherited the estate in 1403. The timber framed gatehouse with a jettied upper storey is rather later, The manor passed to the Habingtons and then to the Barnebys. A new house was built higher up the hillside in the 1760s. The old house has been a National Trust possession since 1946.

LOWER PEDWARDINE MOTTE   SO 367705

A mound 3m high with traces of a ditch and bailey lies 2km south of Brampton Bryan church. Just 0.4km to the NW at Upper Pedwardine (SO 365707) is another mound, partly cut away for farm buildings. There may have been a bailey to the south.

LYDE CASTLE   SO 497439

On a low lying site which was probably once protected by wet moats and marshland are slight traces of a stone castle belonging to one of the knights serving the bishops of Hereford. The castle is mentioned in a document of Henry III's reign.

LYONSHALL CASTLE   SO 331563

It is likely that this castle was founded in the late 11th century by the de Lacys or one of their knights. It is probably one of the two castles belonging to John Devereux which are mentioned in the Pipe Roll for 1188, and it is mentioned as "Lenhaul" in 1209. Stephen Devereux is thought to have erected the circular keep at Lyonshall in c1220-27 in imitation of his overlord Walter de Lacy's new keep at Longtown. During Edward I's reign Lyonshall was the chief seat of William Touchet, and it was held by Bartholomew de Badlesmere at the time of his execution by Edward II in 1322. It later passed by marriage to John de Vere, Earl of Oxford, and from 1386 until his execution in 1388 was held by Sir Simon Burley. Lyonshall then reverted to Sir John Devereux, who in 1391 made a contract with the Hereford mason John Brown for the erection of a hall 13m long by 8m wide with buttressed walls 1m thick. The room was to have four doorways and three large windows including one in a projecting bay with ten lights. Under the same contract Brown was to rebuild the gatehouse with a portcullis and lodgings for a guard. Nothing remains of such structures and Sir John died only two years year, leaving an heiress who married Walter, 5th Baron Fitz-Walter. In 1404 he was ordered by Henry IV to fortify the castle against Owain Glyndwr. From the mid 15th century until 1641 Lyonshall was back in the hands of the Devereux family but there is no evidence that they lived in it and the Thynnes probably inherited a total ruin. They later sold the estate to the Cheese family.

The circular inner bailey, recently partly cleared of undergrowth, lies NE of the church. It measures about 45m in diameter within a curtain wall of which fragments and buried foundations remain. It is surrounded by a wet moat crossed by a wooden bridge to the SE and lies within the SW end of a rectangular outer bailey, whilst there was a third almost square enclosure beyond to the NE. The moats of these outer enclosures are incomplete and now only partly water filled. No stone walls or buildings survive within them. On the north side of the inner bailey the wall projects out as a more thinly walled, but better preserved, polygonal mantlet around the base of a circular tower keep 12.6m in diameter over walls 2.8m thick above a sloping plinth with a roll-moulding at the top. There are three gaps representing basement window loops and a wider gap on the south where the entrance and staircase were.

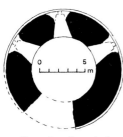

Keep plan, Lyonshall

Lyonshall Castle, remains of keep

MADLEY CASTLE SO 418389

This site 200m NW of the church has been much mutilated, the large 3m high mound being removed in 1963 and the bailey having being mostly obliterated by building works. The platform on the remaining part of the bailey could be the base of a hall block, whilst the mound is likely to have borne a shell keep. To the SW lies an overgrown moated site beyond a housing estate at SO 416386.

MANSELL LACY CASTLE SO 426456

East of Court Farm, SE of the church is an oval platform 33m by 27m with a partly wet moat. The platform has part of a battered plinth of a retaining wall over 2m thick and there are signs of a building inside. There are traces of outworks to the east.

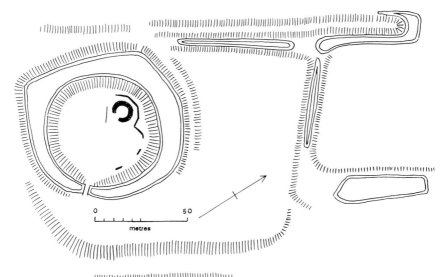

0 50 metres

Plan of Lyonshall Castle

MOCCAS CASTLE   SO 348426

The last traces of this castle vanished a few years ago. It is thought to have had a circular tower keep although the licence to crenellate granted by Edward I to Sir Hugh de Freyne in 1293 specified that the outer wall was not to be more than 3m high to the wall-walk and be without towers or turrets. The property had recently been taken into Crown possession for a short while, possibly because Sir Hugh had illegally begun work on fortifying it without a licence. The Freynes lived here for several generations but in the mid 15th century Edward ap Meredith held Moccas, whilst from the mid 16th century the Vaughans were in possession.

MONNINGTON COURT   SO 382368

Near the house is an oval mound 4m high with partly water-filled ditch. To the west is a crescent-shaped bailey with a ditch formerly filled by a stream. Chapel House to the south is 15th or 16th century and has surrounding earthworks.

MOUSE CASTLE   SO 247424

This hilltop site lies in woodland 1km NE of Cusop. The oval enclosure has steep natural slopes on all sides except to the NE, where there is a double rampart. In the middle is a motte, the earthen slopes of which seem to have been removed to leave the natural rocky core with faces 2m high.

MUCH DEWCHURCH CASTLE   SO 485312

This castle stands on a low ridge with three streams around it. The 3m high mound has a bank on top, possibly the buried base of a wall. Until recently there were traces of a crescent-shaped bailey to the west and there is evidence of two eastern enclosures. Pottery found dated from the 12th century to the 14th century. This castle may well have been finally destroyed by the Welsh in 1402-3.

MUCH MARCLE CASTLE   SO 657329

Just north of the church is a motte rising 6.5m to a summit 30m across on which is assumed to have stood a shell keep, since material from it is said to have been used in the construction of the 15th century central tower of the church, the owner then being Thomas Walwyn. Cottages and gardens occupy a semi-circular bailey to the east and there are two outer enclosures to the NE. Edward I gave the part of Much Marcle which included the castle to Edmund Mortimer, and the church contains a monument to his son Roger's daughter Blanche, wife of Sir Peter de Grandison.

MUNSLEY CASTLE   SO 662408

The 17th century Lower Court lies on a lowered motte which had a wet moat fed by a stream. An L-shaped section of moat to the SW marks a bailey in which are footings of a possible barbican.

MYNYDD-BRITH MOTTE   SO 280415

A ditched oval motte 6m high with a bailey to the west lies SW of the farm. At Nant-y-Bar just 0.5km to the SW at SO 279410 is a ditched motte 3.5m high with a bailey.

Old Castleton Motte

NEWTON TUMP   SO 293441

This low-lying site guards the northern entrance to the Golden Valley. A moated mound 4.5m high stands in one corner of a roughly rectangular bailey now weakly defended but probably once protected with wet moats fed from the Bach Brook. The bailey once had a stone wall 1.5m thick and there seems to have been a SE corner tower a gatehouse on the east and a polygonal building on the mound. A motte was discovered during tree-felling operations at The Bage, just 1km SE at SO 297434.

OLDCASTLE   SO 328520

The damaged motte 5m high stands on the edge of a spur above streams to the east, west and south. A bailey to the north has a platform of a possible hall and a cottage is built in a gap in its rampart. This site is thought to have been the home of Sir John Oldcastle, Lord Cobham, who was executed by Henry V as a heretic in 1417.

OLD CASTLETON   SO 283457

This site consists of a kidney shaped bailey defended by a rampart and ditch and a worn-down motte on the north side. The large outer platform on the east and west are mostly natural and there was once a marsh below to the north. The bailey rampart may be the buried base of a curtain wall.

ORCOP CASTLE   SO 473265

The motte and its kidney shaped bailey to the north are low lying but probably once had wide wet moats filled by the adjacent stream. The mound rises 6.5m to a summit 18m in diameter and the bailey measures about 75m from east to west by 60m from north to south. There are said to be traces of a shell keep on the motte.

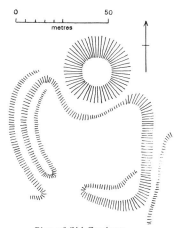

Plan of Old Castleton

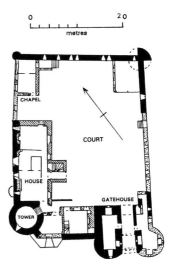

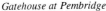

Gatehouse at Pembridge   *Plan of Pembridge Castle*

PEMBRIDGE CASTLE   SO 488193

This castle was originally called Newland and may have been built in King John's reign by Matilda de Braose (nee Valery). It passed to the Pembridge family in 1208 and became their principal seat after their original estate at the village of Pembridge was lost to Roger Mortimer of Wigmore in 1265. However by the mid 14th century their main residence was at Clehonger. In 1387 Sir Richard Burley died in possession of the castle. In 1445 the castle passed to the Hoptons and was later held by the Baynhams, who sold it to Sir Walter Pye. The castle served as an outpost to the Royalist garrison at Monmouth until it was captured after a fortnight's blockade by Colonel Scudamore. A Parliamentary garrison stationed within it was withdrawn in 1646 and the castle then slighted. It was sold to George Kemble and made habitable again. In 1715 it was occupied by Henry Scudamore. It later passed to the Townleys of Lancashire and was then sold to the Baileys, but the occupants during this period were tenant farmers. In the early 20th century the destroyed parts of the gatehouse and curtain walls were rebuilt and new crenellations added upon the walls.

The castle lies on a platform built against a slope so that a substantial outer bank was needed to retain the water of the moat on the NW and NE sides. The building comprises a curtain wall with an average thickness of 1.4m enclosing a rectangular court about 36m long by 27m wide. At the west corner is a four storey round tower thought to date from c1200 and regarded as a keep although it measures only 7.5m in external diameter and is without a staircase, although it is possible there originally was one in a former semi-circular projection on the SE side, as in the keep at Skenfrith. There are several original loops and the third storey has a latrine projecting on the south side, whilst the fireplace on the top storey may also be original. Adjoining this tower was a contemporary hall-block later replaced by a still inhabited early 17th century house with a square stair turret projecting towards the court. Of the same era are the kitchen and larder between the west tower and the gatehouse.

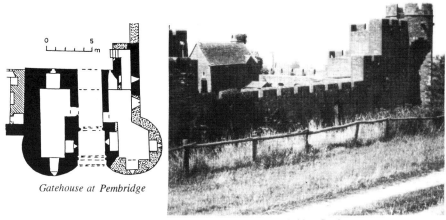

Gatehouse at Pembridge

Pembridge Castle

    The gatehouse and curtain walls are probably of the period c1260-1290. The gate passage was closed by a portcullis and doors and flanked by round towers 6.5m in diameter. The western tower has a rectangular portion of similar width within the court but the much rebuilt eastern tower has a narrower part behind so that the SE curtain wall is flanked by the round part. On the upper storey of the gatehouse is a fireplace of c1400 but most of the rest is 20th century work. The central part of the SE curtain was destroyed in 1646 and the thinner and lower 20th century walling of this part now leaves the house exposed to view from the hillside, which was not originally the case. At the east corner the curtain now steps up to meet a round turret with hollow segments lower down towards the court and on either side of the curtain, a unique way of providing a turret cheaply. The north corner has a tiny round turret and there is the base of another close to the west tower on the NW side. Within the north corner is a 16th century chapel with three 17th century windows pierced through the NW curtain wall. Below it is a tunnel vaulted 13th century cellar.

Pembridge Castle

PEMBRIDGE COURT HOUSE   SO 391580

The original seat of the Pembridge family was a house upon the platform rising 5m above a wet moat immediately SW of Pembridge parish church. The western arm of the moat is now obscured by farm buildings. A castle here is mentioned in 1219 and in the mid 17th century Silas Taylor describes this site as having "remaines of a fortified keep or small castle".

PENYARD CASTLE   SO 618226   V

This castle is first mentioned in 1338 when it was repaired. It was then held by the Talbots and the family may have had a house here as early as Henry II's reign. In the early 15th century it was a residence of Sir Lewis Talbot, son of the Earl of Shrewsbury. There was a mint at the castle in the 16th century. On the death of Gilbert Talbot, 7th Earl of Shrewsbury in 1627 Penyard passed to his daughter Elizabeth, Countess of Kent. A farmhouse was built on part of the site in the late 17th century and there is a record of stone being taken from the demolished castle in the 1690s to built the parsonage house and a barn at Weston-under-Penyard.

The farmhouse is now very ruined and partly choked by debris and vegetation, who also hides the lower parts of a four bay vaulted undercroft 5m wide noted in the 1930s. The only relics of the castle currently visible are a two-light 14th century window reset in the north gable of the farmhouse, now blocked internally, a small fragment of the corner of an ashlar-faced building with walling 1.2m thick to the west, and traces of ditches further west. It is likely that the castle had a rectangular courtyard with the principal apartments overlooking the steep slopes to the south and a gatehouse facing the higher ground to the south.

POSTON CASTLE   SO 358372

The 36m square platform was damaged by ploughing in the 1970s. The manor was held by William de Ecouis at the time of Domesday Book in 1086.

Penyard Castle

RICHARD'S CASTLE   SO 483703   F

This castle is named after Richard Fitz-Scrob, who established a stronghold here c1050. It was held by his son Osbern Fitz-Richard at the time of Domesday Book in 1086. It was then called Avretone (Overton) whilst the adjacent village was called Boiton. Osbern's son Hugh married Eustachia de Say and whilst their eldest son was known as Osbern Fitz-Hugh, his brother Hugh took the surname de Say and inherited the estate in 1185. Hugh was married to Lucia de Clifford, sister of the celebrated Rosamund Clifford and is assumed to have been the builder of the octagonal tower keep on the motte. Their grand-daughter and heiress Margaret de Say married Robert de Mortimer of Burford. In 1264 the castle was seized in the interest of Simon de Montfort. A century later Richard's Castle was divided between heiresses who married members of the Cornwall and Talbot families. The latter seem to have occupied the castle for a while, and Sir Thomas Talbot garrisoned it against Owain Glyndwr, but it was probably little used during the 15th century, and Leland in the 1530s saw it as "going to ruin", and containing just "a poor house of timber in the Castle garth for a farmer". By then the castle was a Crown possession, but in 1545 Henry VIII granted it to the Earl of Warwick. It was later leased to farmers, and since c1600 it has been held by the Salvey family, but at times sublet to the Bradshaws.

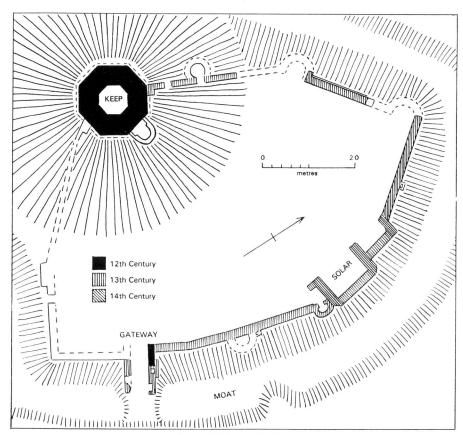

Plan of Richard's Castle

Richard's Castle

The castle has a strong commanding site on a hilltop and consists of a motte with a bailey to the east, beyond which is the churchyard and the site of the former fortified township. When excavated in 1962-4 the top section of the mound proved to be the buried lower storey of an octagonal keep of c1185-1200 with an external diameter of 14.5m over walls 4m thick. Towards the bailey is a slightly later apsidal projection which may have formed a porch, probably with a tiny chapel above. The destroyed inner part of the bailey gatehouse may also have been late 12th century, whilst the curtain wall with traces of three D-shaped towers on the east, north and NW was probably built in the 1220s or 30s. The large residential square tower mostly within the curtain on the east side was probably added in the early 14th century to serve as a solar block for an adjacent hall. The small round tower by the base of the mound on the NW side was converted into a dovecote in the later medieval period when the castle had become no more than a farm. Parts of the NW bailey walls and fragments of the outer parts of the gatehouse stand high but the rest of the walls are mere foundations exposed by the 1960s excavations.

The town may also have had a stone wall and the enclosing bank, which yielded 11th or 12th century pottery, was linked to the wall of the castle bailey by a stone wall in the 13th century. Traces of a 13th century bastion, later converted into a dovecote, were found on the east. Further south is the detached church tower of c1300 set overlooking the approach east of the chancel rather than at the more usual position west of the nave, where a high embattled tower would have hindered defence of the castle. An enquiry of 1364 on the death of Hugh Mortimer shows that the town then had 103 burgages, a market and a fair having being granted to it by King John in 1216. The town subsequently declined and Leland records only two farms and three or four cottages as remaining on the hilltop.

ROSS PALACE   SO 597243

Richard's Castle

The bishops of Hereford had a palace or manor house at Ross, which seems to have been regarded as a defensible structure in 1166-7 when the Pipe Rolls refer to it being provisioned. The cellars of a later medieval house have been found below the Royal Hotel which lies on a good defensive site on the west side of the town close to the medieval looking round tower and walls of the early 19th century dominating the view here.

ROWLESTONE MOTTE   SO 375272

To the NE of the church is a motte 4.5m high. The 14th century buildings of Court Farm lie on the likely site of the bailey.

ST DEVEREUX MOTTE   SO 451320

The buildings of the early 16th century Didley Court Farm lie beside a 5m high mound thought to have once borne a shell keep. There are traces of a crescent-shaped bailey to the north and another enclosure to the west.

ST MARGARET'S MOTTE   SO 358339

A small mound up to 3m high lies ENE of the church.

ST WEONARD'S MOTTE   SO 497243

South of the church is an overgrown mound rising 5m to a summit 23m across into which a cutting was made in 1855. Originally a burial mound, it was adapted as a motte and possibly once bore a shell keep. A bailey to the south has been obliterated by new roads and buildings.

SHOBDON CASTLE   SO 399628

West of the church is a motte rising 3m high to a summit 45m across with traces of foundations. A chicken processing factory lies on the site of a bailey to the east which probably had a wet moat originally. The castle was probably built by Oliver Merlymond, tenant of Shobdon under Hugh de Mortimer and instigator of the building of the fine Norman church of which three reset arches stand on the hill above. There is another possible castle site to the east at SO 408628, and there is also a 3m high mound at SO 402627 by the drive up to Shobdon Court 250m south of the church.

SNODHILL CASTLE   SO 322404

Robert de Chandos probably built this castle after acquiring the land by an exchange with Great Malvern Priory in 1127. The castle is mentioned in the Pipe Rolls for 1196 and it was probably about that time that it was refortified in stone. When Roger de Chandos died c1355 the castle was surveyed and found to be ruinous. The large tower SW of the motte may have been part of a subsequent remodelling. Sir John Chandos was ordered by Henry IV to fortify the castle against the rebel Welsh in 1403. After his death in 1428 Snodhill passed to Giles Bruges but in 1436 was held by Richard de la Mere, Sheriff of Herefordshire. It later passed to the Nevilles and seems to have been little used since Leland describes it as "somewhat in ruine". Elizabeth I granted Snodhill to her favourite Robert Dudley, Earl of Leicester, and the estate later passed to the Vaughans. In 1665 they sold it to William Prosser of London, who built or rebuilt Snodhill Court, using material from the castle, which had been wrecked by a bombardment by an army under the Earl of Leven in 1645. The whereabouts of the castle chapel, which was repaired after destruction by the Welsh in c1404 and remained in use up to the Civil War period, is not known.

The keep on the motte was an unusual form of hall-keep of elongated octagonal shape, measuring 11.5m long by 7m wide within walls 2m thick at the level of the low basement. The walls were considerably thinner above an offset to carry the hall floor. The two fragments now remaining more than 1m high show a narrow basement loop, the jamb of a hall south window and one side of the entrance with a draw-bar slot behind a door rebate. Later in the 13th century flanking round turrets were added in front of the entrance with a portcullis between them.

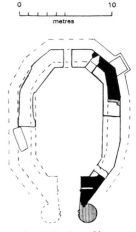

0   10
metres

Snodhill Castle

Snodhill: plan of keep

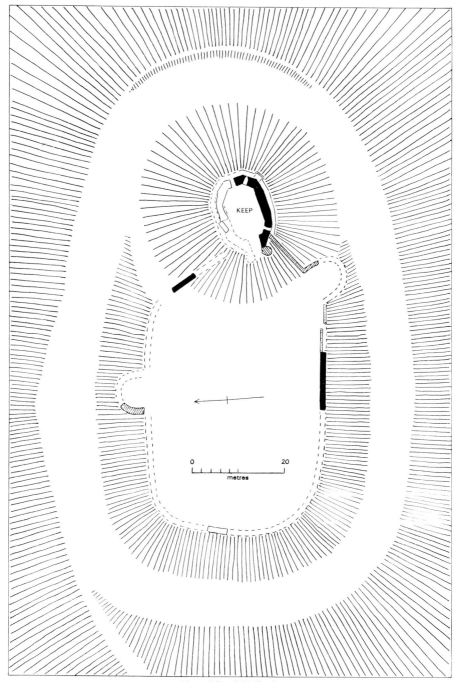

Plan of Snodhill Castle

The bailey at Snodhill extends for 60m to the west of the keep and is 40m wide. Part of a curtain wall 2m thick survives to about 1.5m high on the south side and there there are smaller fragments at the west end and on the NE, ascending the mound slope, where the wall was thinner. On the north side is a high fragment of a D-shaped tower containing polygonal rooms which possibly acted as a solar block to an adjacent hall. At the SE corner is an U-shaped tower of some size with thin walling of possibly 17th century date connecting it to the south curtain. It is likely there were other towers at the west corners and a gatehouse on the NE beside the mound, whilst there is a large outer bailey at a lower level to the east.

SOLLARS HOPE   SO 613333

At Court Farm is a low mound at the junction of two streams. The stonework on the top may be remnants of pigsties only recently demolished.

STAPLETON CASTLE   SO 323656

Stapleton was held by Osbern Fitz-Richard in 1086 but the earthworks are thought to date from the mid 1140s, when Osbern Fitz-Hugh lost the castle at Presteigne to Roger Port and built a castle here to replace it. It later passed to the Says and is mentioned in 1207 during the minority of Margaret de Say, after which it passed by marriage to the Mortimers of Richard's Castle. In 1304 Stapleton passed to the Cornewalls ahnd on the orders of Henry IV the castle was garrisoned against the rebel Welsh by Sir John Cornewall. He led a force of archers and men-at-arms within Henry V's army at Agincourt in 1415 and for many years trophies captured during the campaign were displayed in the castle. In the early 17th century a large H-plan house was built within the former shell keep, which was cut down to form retaining wall to support the basement. Medieval latrine shutes survive on the west side and in the right-angled SE corner. The later house is now very ruined but the east and east walls of the main block and parts of the SW and NE wings still remain, the latter incorporating a thicker section of walling on the north side with one side of the original shell keep entrance with a draw-bar slot. There is a ditch on all sides except the south, where the ground falls away very steeply, and a D-shaped bailey extends beyond the ditch about 50m to the north. It also seems to have had stone curtain wall. The house is said to have been "defaced" by Sir Michael Woodhouse in 1645 to prevent Parliamentary troops occupying it. In 1706 the Cornwalls sold Stapleton to the Harleys, who repaired and occupied the house, the east facing windows with brick arches being their work.

STAUNTON-ON-ARROW MOTTE   SO 369600

The motte rises 8m from a wet moat to a summit 19m across. The church to the east lies in one of several outer enclosures.

STOKE CROSS MOTTE   SO 625505

An overgrown moated mound 2m high lies 1.5km NNE of Stoke Lacy church.

STRETFORD MOTTE   SO 444555

South of the church is a hillock on a ridge with traces of a bailey rampart. The paddock below is called Castle Green. There is stone in the adjacent Chapel Field.

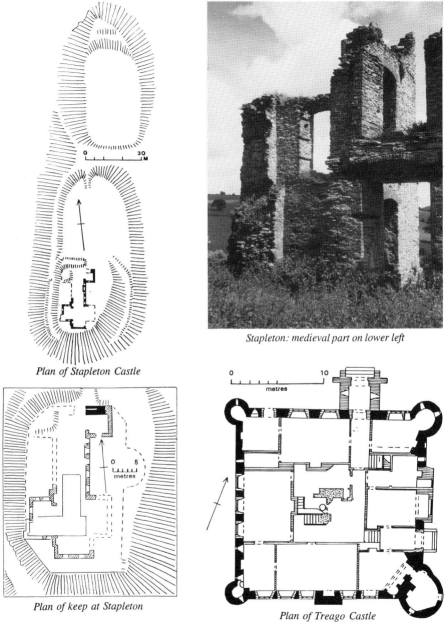

Stapleton: medieval part on lower left

Plan of Stapleton Castle

Plan of keep at Stapleton

Plan of Treago Castle

THRUXTON MOTTE   SO 436346

By Thruxton Court Farm is a small but steeply sided motte on which is a small stone chamber, possibly a well-shaft since it was once used as a water tank.

Treago Castle

TREAGO CASTLE   SO 490239

Treago has long been the seat of the Mynors family. John de Mynors may have had a fortified house here in the time of Edward II but none of the present buildings appear to be older than the 1490s. The site is a shelf of land commanded by rising ground to the west and it is assumed there was once a wet moat. The house is roughly a square of about 20m within walls 1m thick. There were thinly walled ranges of rooms set around a court 7.6m square. Originally the kitchen lay in the south range and the entrance was in the middle of the east range where there is a much rebuilt shallow projection. Probably the hall lay in the west range, although one description says it was in the north range, where a fine late-medieval roof still survives. Round turrets about 2.6m in external diameter project from the western corners, whilst the NE and SE corners have larger turrets of 3.7m and 5m external diameter containing rooms. These turrets have cross-loops suitable for handguns flanking the main walls, in which are several typical Early Tudor type windows with pairs of four-centred-headed lights under square heads. The turrets rise one level above the two storeys of the main ranges and are covered with conical roofs. The SE tower had a spiral stair built into the junction with the south wall and has a projecting topmost storey built in the late 18th century. The existing doorway in the east range is mid-16th century and of the same period is the present main entrance in the north front with a buttressed three storey porch. The roofs of the ranges are mostly of the late 16th century whilst the upper rooms were much altered in the 17th century. The castle fell into decay when let out as a farm in the early 19th century and alterations made during the restoration of the 1840s included filling in the courtyard to provide a central hall to contain a new main staircase.

TREGATE CASTLE   SO 480171

Above the River Monnow is a large motte 3.5m high with a rampart on top covering the footings of a shell keep. There are signs of outer enclosures damaged by the erection of farm buildings.

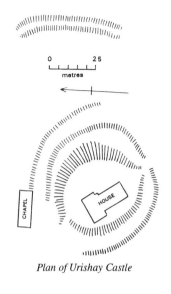

Plan of Urishay Castle

Urishay Castle

TRETIRE CASTLE   SO 521238

South of a house by the church is a platform with a ditch and rampart on the north side. The rampart may conceal remains of stone wall and towers built in the early 13th century by Fulke Fitz-Warine, lord of the Shropshire castles of Alberbury and Whittington. Foundations were traced in the 19th century. In 1292 there was a dispute over possession of the castle between John Tregoz and Walter de Huntley.

TURNASTONE RINGWORK   SO 357365

This is the site of a ploughed-out ringwork. Cothill Tump at SO 338363 has a ditched mound 3.5m high but investigation suggested it was a Bronze Age burial site.

UPTON BISHOP MOTTE   SO 652281

At Castle Tump Field, which has produced pottery from the early 12th century to the 14th century, is a worn down motte rising 3.5m above its ditch and an almost ploughed-out bailey.

URISHAY CASTLE   SO 323376   V

The estate was originally called Hay and the first part of the name refers to Ulric, the tenant here in the 12th century under the Mortimers. A ruined 17th and 18th century house possibly incorporating medieval masonry either reset or in situ lies on the west side of the summit of a large motte 6.5m high with a surrounding ditch, once crossed by a bridge on the NE side. A bailey ditch is visible beyond the former tennis courts to the west, and there is a Norman chapel on the north edge of the motte ditch. The house was inhabited until the early 20th century.

WACTON MOTTE   SO 614576

The 17th century house called The Court has a partly wet moat which incorporates part of the ditch of the bailey of a 3.5m high oval motte 70m to the north. It is thought that this mound bore a circular keep and that the bailey was also walled.

WALFORD MOTTE   SO 391724

A small mound rising 5m to a top 11m across with traces of possible stonework lies in former marshland between two tributaries of the River Teme. A bailey on the east has remains of a wet moat but is encroached upon by a farm. Another bailey lay to the NE. Pottery dating from the 13th to the 14th century has come from this site. A moated site of some size lies to the west at SO 383723.

WALLINGSTONES MOAT   SO 503222

There is little to see now but much is known of this site since it was excavated between 1959 and 1963. It is probably named after a 12th century tenant Roger Fit Walding, and in the late 15th and early 16th centuries it was held by the Maynston family. By the mid 13th century there was a block containing a hall with a corner latrine over an undercroft. A mound was raised against it and a wing added at the higher level of the mound summit. The building was partly demolished in the mid 14th century and in the 15th century a new house was built on the north edge of the mound and the old undercroft filled with rubbish. A curtain wall was then built around the base of the mound. The site was robbed of its materials after c1600.

WALTERSTONE CASTLE   SO 339250

West of the church is a mound rising 9m to a summit 10m across. The southern part of the ditch still contains water. To the east, NE and south are traces of mostly ploughed-out bailey platforms. This site is thought to have been abandoned by 1137.

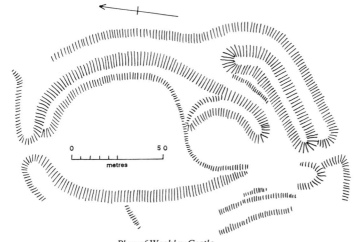

Plan of Weobley Castle

Weobley Castle

WEOBLEY CASTLE   SO 403513   F

This castle was built by the de Lacys in the late 11th century. In 1138 it was fortified by Geoffrey Talbot against King Stephen who besieged and captured the castle. In 1208 the castle was the base of William de Braose during his rebellion against King John and from it he sallied out to burn the town of Leominster. The castle was then a possession of Walter de Lacy, who had wide possessions in Ireland and the Welsh Marches and had married Matilda de Braose c1200. Walter was all-powerful in Herefordshire in the period 1216-23 when he was sheriff of the county and responsible for its defence against the Welsh. It is most likely that the now-vanished walls and towers at Weobley were constructed during that period. Walter's son Gilbert and grandson Walter died before his own death in 1241 at which Weobly passed to his daughter Margaret, who married John de Verdon. In 1388 Weobly passed to the Devereux family who became earls of Essex in Elizabeth I's reign. After the last earl died in 1646 Weobley passed by marriage to the Dukes of Somerset and then to the Thynne family. Leland describes the castle as decayed and it was probably little used during the 16th and 17th centuries.

The castle earthworks lie on flat ground at the south end of the village. They comprise a ringwork with an oval bailey 65m wide extending 75m to the north. There is a strong outer bank to the south and the whole was surrounded by water-filled moats. The ringwork is badly damaged but the eastern part may survive to about the original height. It measured about 30m across the top of the rampart. The bailey still has an impressive east rampart probably with foundations buried within it, but any rampart that existed on the west side has now vanished.

A very interesting plan of the stone buildings made in 1655 by Silas Taylor has survived. It is evidently diagrammatical rather than an accurate survey but it indicates that there were six round towers flanking the outer walls, a gateway at the north end, and on or within the ringwork a rectangular tower keep with four round corner towers. North of this keep stood a pair of domestic buildings.

WHITNEY CASTLE   SO 272465

This castle was the seat of the Whitney family descended from Turstin the Fleming, who held land here in Henry I's reign. In 1675 the existence of a former stone tower was still remembered by locals. The site was destroyed in 1730 when the River Wye suddenly changed its course and washed it away.

Wigmore Castle

WIGMORE CASTLE   SO 408693   F

Wigmore was one of the castles founded by William Fitz-Osbern in 1067-70. After the forfeiture of his son Roger de Breteuil in 1075 it was granted to Ralph de Mortimer, being mentioned as his chief seat in the Domesday Book of 1086. Hugh de Mortimer was a strong supporter of King Stephen and in 1155 the castle was captured by the recently crowned Henry II, who mistrusted Hugh. The small mound near the church may be a siege-work from this period. Forces loyal to Richard I captured it from his son Roger when the latter supported Prince John's rebellion in 1191. Henry III granted Roger's son Hugh 20 marks towards strengthening the castle against Llywelyn ab Iorwerth in 1223. It is assumed to have been attacked by Simon de Montfort in 1264, since Roger Mortimer III supported King Henry III, but it was evidently in Mortimer hands in May 1265 when Prince Edward sought refuge here after his escape from captivity by de Montfort at Hereford.

The castle must have had stone defences by the time of the 1191 siege but the existing walls and towers mostly date from a rebuilding by Roger Mortimer IV in the early 14th century. Roger joined the Bohuns and other Marcher lords in opposition to the Despencers, the widely-despised favourites of Edward II. In 1322 he was forced to submit to King Edward and was imprisoned in the Tower of London. The castle is then recorded as containing three siege engines called springalds, plus six tents and supplies of arms and armour. With the assistance of Bishop Orleton of Hereford he managed to escape and flee to France where he became the ally and lover of King Edward's estranged queen, Isabella. In 1326 they returned to England, deposed and imprisoned the king and ruled in the name of the teenage Edward III until in 1330 the latter took over the reigns of government after arresting and executing Earl Roger at Nottingham. Wigmore was then granted to William Montacute, Earl of Salisbury, and Roger Mortimer V only regained his father's estates and earldom of March created in 1328 by marrying Montacute's heiress in 1354.

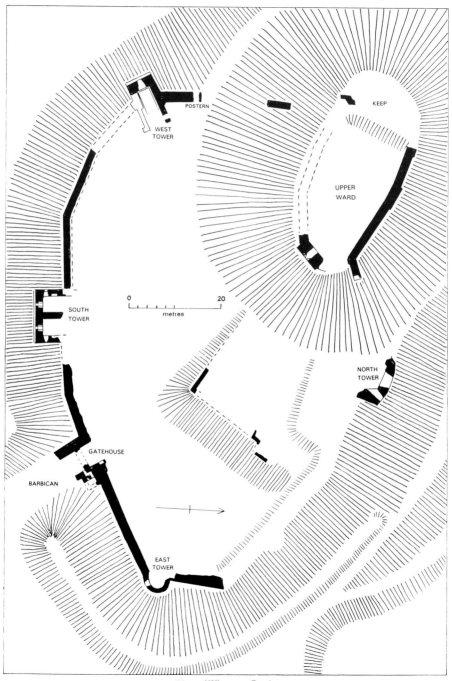

Plan of Wigmore Castle

On the death of Edmund, 5th Earl of March in 1425 his honours and estates passed to Richard, Duke of York, a great-grandson of Edward III and the son of the heiress Anne Mortimer. Richard became involved in a power struggle against the weak Henry VI and the Beaufort Dukes of Somerset. Richard was killed at the battle of Wakefield in December 1460 but his son won victories at Mortimer's Cross near Wigmore and Towton in Yorkshire early in 1461 and then seized the throne as Edward IV. By this time Wigmore had been eclipsed in importance by the palatial neighbouring castle of Ludlow. However it remained inhabited and the noted Parliamentarian Sir Robert Harley was born within it, his father Thomas having purchased the castle. In 1643 the Harleys, who lived in the nearby castle of Brampton Bryan, dismantled the fortifications at Wigmore to prevent the site being occupied by Royalists.

The castle is impressively and strongly sited on a ridge, through which a very deep and wide ditch was cut to the west beyond the motte. East of the motte is a square platform on which it appears there were palatial apartments, at least from the 14th century, although very little now remains of them, whilst below to the east and south is a spacious bailey 100m long from east to west with a ditch and outer bank facing the approach from the SE. Projections on the outer side of this bank suggest the possibility of an outer wall here flanked by round bastions, although no stonework remains visible. Although considerable conservation of the ruins has been undertaken by English Heritage in the 1990s the bailey is still quite heavily overgrown except for a network of paths. Much of the circuit of the walls around the east and south sides of the bailey still remains in a very ruined state, but there is a gap on the west and a long stretch on the NE which is missing together with a possible D-shaped tower similar to the east tower, which is 5.5m in diameter over walls just 0.9m thick, and thought to be 13th century. A latrine adjoins it to the north. On the south side is the rectangular south tower 11.8m wide containing two pleasant rooms with fireplaces and seats in the window embrasures at courtyard level and a single large chamber above. Between here and the east tower is the gatehouse, a structure 8.4m wide but of unknown length since the outer and inner parts are missing. The half-buried pointed arch lay about half way along the gateway passage. An account of 1872 suggests there were inner and outer portcullises worked from chambers above. The passage in the east wall led to a latrine in a projection. The SW tower was a long narrow structure with two single rooms set over a dark basement. As with the south tower the outer parts stand high but none of the inner parts stand above courtyard level. North of this tower the head of a mostly-buried postern gate is visible. The north tower is a wide polygon towards the field and may have formed a solar block serving an adjacent hall.

On the mound summit are the remains of walls 2m thick enclosing a court 20m wide by nearly 40m long. Much of the north wall still stands 7m high and has a shallow but broad projection in the middle. The lower part of this section may be 12th century work. To the SE is another shallow projection with a 14th century window embrasure in it. It is likely there was always an access to the summit between these parts but the Buck brothers' print shows an entrance on the south side, where the wall is now reduced to just buried footings. On the west is a high fragment of walling with evidence of a staircase and the jambs of several windows. This seems to have formed part of an irregularly shaped octagonal tower keep about 13m across, probably of the 1320s and likely to have had a latrine projection facing south. It is greatly to be regretted that English Heritage did not excavate this part of the site for the basement of this potentially very interesting building almost certainly survives about 5m high under the mound of debris.

Gatehouse at Wigmore

WILLEY LODGE   SO 336692

It has been suggested that the foundations by a house on a promontory belong to a small tower keep.

Window, south tower, Wigmore   *East tower, Wigmore*

Wilton Castle

WILTON CASTLE   SO 590244   V

This castle was of strategic importance since it guarded one of the few bridges over the River Wye. It seems to have originally been a motte and bailey site and is mentioned by Giraldus Cambrensis and in the Pipe Rolls for 1188 and 1204-6, then being held by Hugh Longchamp. It later passed to William Fitz-Hugh and then by marriage to Roger de Grey, who rebuilt the castle in stone at the end of the 13th century. It probably fell into decay during the 15th century and in the late 16th century the southern part of the building was replaced by a new house built by the Brydges family. Sir John Brydges, who died in 1651, tried to remain neutral in the Civil War and went off to serve in Ireland but, although there is evidence that the castle was not regarded as tenable as a fortress, it was burnt one Sunday whilst the family were at church, the instigator being Sir John's brother-in-law Barnaby Scudamore, Royalist governor of Hereford. The ruins were sold in 1722 to Guy's hospital in London but in 1784 the ancient title of Lord Grey of Wilton was revived and granted to Sir Thomas Egerton, and an earldom of Wilton was created in 1801. At the end of the 19th century parts of the ruins were patched up to make a new house which remains habitable and was sold to local fruit farmers in the 1990s.

The original motte probably lay at the SE corner, commanding the bridge, which in its present form is late 16th century. The walls around this section have vanished but most of the rest of the enceinte remains in a ruinous condition. except for a gap filled by a thin low modern wall east of the NW tower. The long U-shaped structure 10m wide at the SW corner is thought to have been the solar block with a retainers hall beneath it. The round west end with a latrine projecting high up on the west side is ruined, while the eastern part is incorporated in the modern house and has a wide staircase down to the lower hall and remains of a narrower stair up to the solar. It is likely that there was a twin-towered gatehouse adjoining this block to the east, where ruins of the late 16th century house now stand. North of the solar block was the great hall, for which there are window embrasures in the west curtain wall. Beyond it presumably lay the service rooms. The octagonal NW tower measures 6m across and had three storeys of rooms with fireplaces and latrines in a projection on the east side. It may be of later date than the rest of the defences. The badly cracked east tower is circular with a diameter of 7.6m although it has a straight side where it joins the curtain wall, in which is a latrine. The NE tower is too ruined for its size and shape to be determined and just the straight wall towards the court now remains.

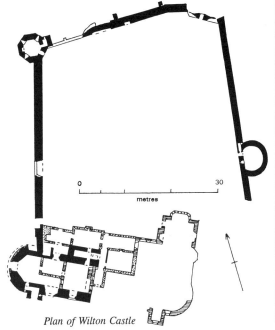

Plan of Wilton Castle

East tower at Wilton

LIST OF MOATED SITES IN HEREFORDSHIRE

BIRCHEND SO 666447 A moat lies close to the house.
BIRLEY SO 455534 Moat opposite church mostly filled in by the 1990s.
BISHOPSTONE SO 416440 Stone lined rectangular moat west of the court.
BODENHAM SO 528510 The Devereux family seat at Moat House was moated.
BOLSTONE SO 547323 Moat in Trilloes Court Wood.
BROCKBURY SO 746419 Part of a triangular moat remains north of the house.
BRYNGWYN SO 484306 Rectangular wet moat beside a farm track.
BURGHILL SO 478445 A moat west of the church has now been filled in.
CANON FROME SO 645436 Court was formerly moated. Involved in Civil War.
CHENEY COURT SO 669477 House gone except barn. Is said to have been moated.
CLOUDS SO 592381 Earthwork in plantation near stream.
COTTS FARM SO 474512 Moat 200m north of farm now filled in.
COURT OF NOKE SO 372595 Slight traces of former moat.
COURT-Y-PARK SO 646397 House on mound. Slight evidence of former moat.
CUMMIN'S FARM SO 738410 Part of moat remains on north side of house.
DONNINGTON SO 708342 Moat south of church is still partly wet.
FORD SO 564585 Part of square moat remains south of the house.
FREENS COURT SO 523459 Tudor house demolished 1957. Fragment of moat.
FREETOWN SO 635420 Part of a wet moat survives by a farm.
GATLEY FARM SO 449686 Moat around 17th century house now gone.
GOBBETS SO 330404 Site of possible hall block on bank of River Dore.
HAYE PARK SO 492724 Rectangular moat in woodland.
HELL MOAT SO 366520 Dry earthwork in woodland.

HINTON SO 574473 Pool by farm is former moat with platform removed.
HOPE MANSELL SO 624199 Slight traces of moat around Moat Farm.
HOPTON SO 668471 One dry arm of wide moat remains north of farmhouse.
KINSHAM SO 362645 Moat around Lower Court House nearly filled in.
LANGSTONE COURT SO 536219 Rectangular wet moat SE of the Court.
LAWTON'S HOPE SO 472502 50m square moated platform with stream on north.
LEDICOT SO 415623 There are now no remains of this moat.
LEOMINSTER SO 499584 Rectangular moat once lay 750m south of priory church.
LITTLE SARNESFIELD SO 388522 Rectangular moat with causeway on north side.
LODGE FARM SO 387694 Oval moated platform 24m across NNE of farm.
LORD'S WOOD SO 555150 Triangular moat 2km south of Whitchurch.
LOWER HOPTON SO 632493 Circular moat near the farmhouse.
LOWER LYDE SO 519440 North angle of moat remains at 17th century house.
LUGWARDINE SO 550413 Large dry moat not far north of the church.
MAINSTONE COURT SO 658398 Irregular shaped platform within wide wet moat.
MARTIN'S CASTLE SO 649604 Rectangular moat close to B4214.
MATHON SO 734457 Oval moat west of Church Farm.
MEER COURT SO 438364 Part of wet moat remains SW of the Court.
MOAT FARM SO 747447 Moat NW of 17th century house.
MOOR ABBEY SO 545633 Fragment of moat beside house. Fishpond beyond.
MOREHAMPTON PARK SO 377341 Traces of former moat around the farm.
MORETON ON LUGG SO 504456 South and west arms remain of a wet moat.
NETHER COURT SO 620494 Tennis court lies on site of former moated platform.
NETHERWOOD SO 634608 Farm was once a rectangular moated mansion.
NEW HOUSE SO 645445 One arm of a moat remains to the SE of the house.
NUNSLAND SO 379538 Wet moat SE of the house. NW side is obliterated.
OLDCASTLE SO 754407 Platform has now been removed from wet moat.
OLD LONGWORTH SO 564393 17th century house with traces of moat.
PAUNCEFORD COURT SO 674406 The dry east arm of the moat still remains.
PIXLEY SO 6622389 Moat once enclosed both house and church.
ROWDEN ABBEY SO 632564 House went in 18th century. Part of moat remains.
RUSHALL SO 642348 An oval moat has now been obliterated.
ST DEVEREUX SO 439302 Square moat now mostly filled in.
SAWBURY HILL SO 626553 Gone now, but traces remained a century ago.
SEED FARM SO 704476 Oval moat around the house.
SHOWLE COURT SO 612437 Fragment of wet moat remains to south of house.
SHUCKNALL SO 587424 Only a small pool survives of the moat.
STOKE LACY SO 620493 Two arms remain of a wet moat near a house.
TARRINGTON SO 616405 A fragment of a moat survives at the Court.
TEMPLE COURT SO 691433 This Templar preceptory was once moated.
TRELOUGH SO 432312 The moat round the house is now mostly filled in.
ULLINGSWICK SO 590495 A square moat lies 700m WSW of the church.
UPLEADON SO 668419 Slight traces of a moat remain in an orchard.
WALSOPTHORNE SO 650424 Only fragments now remain of the moat.
WESTHIDE COURT SO 587442 Fragment of dry moat to north of house.
WETTON SO 373537 The pool is a relic of a former moat.
WHITBOURNE SO 726568 Oval moat in garden of house. Filled in on NW.
YARKHILL SO 608425 Rectangular moat with very overgrown platform.
YELD SO 351563 Filled in 1970, now garden. Medieval pottery found.

About a dozen other moats are mentioned in the gazetteer entries, mostly in conjunction with other nearby earthworks.

INTRODUCTION TO WORCESTERSHIRE CASTLES

In contrast to Herefordshire the county of Worcester has one of the lowest concentrations of castles in England, although there are plenty of the ordinary domestic moated sites, with good examples at Astwood Court, Earl's Croome, Harvington Hall and Throckmorton. The county lies some distance from any coastline or contentious border subject to raids and an unusually high proportion of the manors within it were held by the four great Benedictine monastic houses at Evesham, Great Malvern, Pershore and Worcester. Some of their granges were moated, as were some of the manor house of the bishops of Worcester. Only at Hartlebury did the bishops have a proper quadrangular moated castle with corner towers and a gatehouse in addition to fine apartments, although their palace beside the cathedral at Worcester was also a licensed embattled building.

A royal motte and bailey castle was raised at Worcester soon after the Norman Conquest. It was partly refortified in stone in King John's reign, only to be dismantled early in Henry III's reign. John built a fortified hunting lodge at Hanley which later passed to the de Clares and the Despencers before being dismantled for its materials in Henry VIII's reign.

From the early 12th century until the mid 15th century the principal baronial family in Worcestershire were the Beauchamps. They had a substantial castle at Elmley on the side of Bredon Hill with two baileys with a rectangular tower keep on the crosswall between them, but from the mid 13th century they preferred to reside at the more accessible castle at Warwick, which they later developed into a fine palace, and Elmley was left to decay. The Beauchamps also briefly had a castle at Bengeworth and in the 1380s another branch of the family built an embattled house at Holt. The only other baronial castles were the motte and bailey strongholds at Castlemorton, Ham or Homme and Leigh, a castle of uncertain date and form at Beoley, a castle at Shrawley which seems to have been a smaller copy of Hartlebury, and fortified houses at Inkberrow and Strensham of which only moats now remain.

Hartlebury became the principal castle in Worcestershire after the demise of that at Worcester and Elmley's eclipse by Warwick. It and the house at Strensham were both held for King Charles during the Civil War and their walls and towers were mostly demolished afterwards. Much altered domestic apartments and moats remain at Hartlebury. Elmley has considerable earthworks and buried foundations, whilst just a single tower remains as part of a later house at Holt. The de Somery castles of Dudley and Weoley once lay in Worcestershire but are now in the West Midlands County. Dudley is described in the Staffordshire volume of this series, and Weoley in the Warwickshire volume.

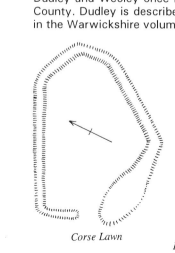

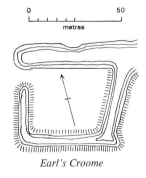

0   50
metres

Earl's Croome

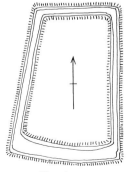

Throckmorton

Corse Lawn

Plans of moated sites in Worcestershire

GAZETTEER OF CASTLES IN WORCESTERSHIRE

ALVECHURCH MOAT   SP 032726

The site of the manor house of the bishops of Worcester is now only represented by two adjacent moated platforms set above gullies in which run the River Arrow and a tributary stream. One platform is about 54m square and is still entirely surrounded by water held in by a strong outer bank to the SW and SE. The other platform is the same width and extends for about 80m to the NE. A house lies in the NE corner of the latter, where the moat has been filled in. Leland describes the house as being a timber structure of recent construction which had just been repaired by Bishop Latimer. The form of the building in which Bishop Blois died in 1236, and which was much used by Bishop Giffard, is uncertain, but it may never have been of stone. Parliament sold off the house in 1648 but it was restored to the bishops in the 1660s. It was destroyed in 1780 and in 1860 the see gave the site to the Ecclesiastical Commissioners.

BENGEWORTH CASTLE   SP 041437

Bengeworth was held by Urse D'Abitot at the time of Domesday Book in 1086 but appears to have been his successors the Beauchamps who raised a castle here beside a bridge of the River Severn during King Stephen's reign. During those lawless years Walter de Beauchamp raised nearby Evesham Abbey, for which he was excommunicated, and the forces of Abbot William de Andeville occupied and then destroyed the castle, a cemetery being created on the site. The Beauchamps officially gave the site to the abbey in 1268. The moat was still visible in the 19th century.

BEOLEY CASTLE   SP 066694

A spur commanding an extensive view has a ditch around the summit creating a quite strongly defended oval area measuring over 100m from SW to NE by 85m wide. This may be the site of the Beauchamps' house accidentally burnt down in 1303, but replaced by 1316 when a court and grange are recorded as existing.

CASTLEMORTON MOTTE   SO 795371

South of the church is an oval mound about 6m high standing in the southern half of a bailey. The castle appears to have been built in King Stephen's reign by the Folliotts. They sold Castlemorton to Richard de Berking, Abbot of Westminster from 1222 to 1246, who is recorded as having a chapel and chaplain here. The castle is last heard of in Edward I's reign.

Elmley Castle

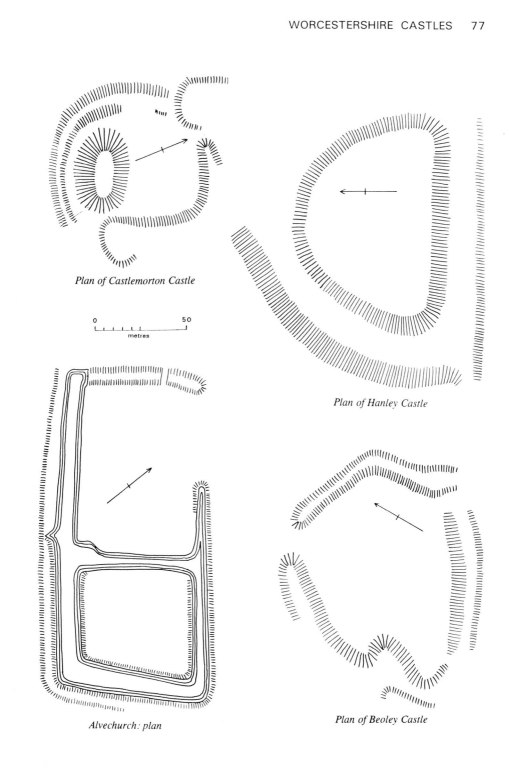

Plan of Castlemorton Castle

0 _____ 50
        metres

Plan of Hanley Castle

Alvechurch: plan

Plan of Beoley Castle

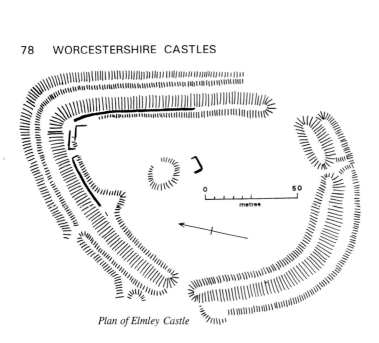

Plan of Elmley Castle

ELMLEY CASTLE   SO 989403

Shortly after the time of the Domesday survey of 1086 a castle was built at Elmley by Robert D'Abitot. It passed to his brother Urso, Sheriff of Worcestershire. His son Roger was disinherited for slaying a royal messenger and Elmley passed via his daughter Emmeline to her husband Walter Beauchamp. His son William was in possession during the wars of King Stephen's reign, during which the castle was probably strengthened and perhaps first fortified in stone.

In 1234 Walter Beauchamp enclosed a park below the castle and stocked it with ten does and three bucks donated by Henry III. Elmley was then the foremost castle in Worcestershire, having superseded that at Worcester. However, William Beauchamp, who died in 1269, married Isabel, sister and heiress of William Mauduit, Earl of Warwick, and in 1267 their son William inherited the castle and earldom of Warwick. The latter was more conveniently sited and the family soon transferred there from the hilltop stronghold at Elmley. By 1316 a survey found the castle at Elmley so far out of repair that it was regarded as worth nothing. Minor repairs may have been made later but in 1540 the castle was said to be "uncovered and in decay", and about the same time Leland saw only one tower left standing and watched stone from the ruins being carted off to rebuild the bridge at Pershore.

The castle was built within the eastern portion of an Iron Age hillfort set on a strong and commanding site high up on the north side of Bredon Hill. The castle has high ramparts and deep ditches around a pear-shaped area 150m long by 100m wide. The base of a curtain wall about 1.6m thick is exposed on the north and lies buried in the rampart on the south. In the middle is part of what may be part of the base of the forebuilding which protected the side of the tower keep which contained the entrance high above ground level. This keep seems to have been set on the line of a wall dividing off the northern end as an inner bailey. In the 13th century there would have been extensive domestic and service buildings scattered around within the two courts but nothing remains visible of them. Some excavations were carried out in the 1930s and it was probably then than some of the walls now visible were uncovered, but unfortunately the war intervened before a report could be published.

Elmley Castle

HANLEY CASTLE   SO 838414

Hanley Castle was built in 1207-12 by King John as a hunting lodge at a cost of nearly £750. He was there in 1209 and 1213, and assizes were held at the castle in 1211-12. Early in his reign Henry III granted the castle to Gilbert de Clare. After the last Gilbert de Clare was killed at the battle of Bannockburn in 1314 the castle passed his his sister Eleanor to her husband Hugh le Despencer. In 1321-2 the castle was damaged by the rebel barons who hated the favoured Despencers. Hugh was executed in 1326 after Edward II was deposed, and Roger Mortimer, Earl of March briefly had possession in 1330, but he in turn was executed in that year. Hanley was then returned to the widowed Eleanor de Clare, who was living in the castle in c1349 when extensions were made to improve the accommodation.

In 1416 Eleanor, widow of Richard le Despencer, was granted the use of the following parts of the castle: "a great room at the end of the hall to the west with two towers of stone annex'd the said hall with one third of the pantry and buttery under the said room....two rooms called le guesten chambres, three towers in the south of the castle with a fourth tower in a corner of the castle....a third of the bakehouse and kitchen adjacent to said tower....with a third of the palisade and moat around the castle". She also had use of the chapel, a third of the garden of the manor and a third of the park, but had to pay a third of the constable's fees. Evidently the castle was then an extensive building with many chambers.

Hanley Castle later passed by marriage to the earls of Warwick. Repairs to the chapel, mill, kitchen, gatehouse and drawbridge are recorded in the 1480s. Henry VII had the young new Earl of Warwick executed in 1499 as a dangerous rival and then retained the castle, giving custody of it to Sir John Savage. In Henry VIII's reign the custodian was Sir William Crompton, who dismantled the building for its materials. Leland refers to him as having "clene defacid it yn his tyme".

Later in the 16th century Hanley Castle was owned by Roland Badger. Although Habington in the 17th century commented that the "castell is so vanished as theare appeareth nothinge in that place but a littel rubbyshe and a silly barn", and the Badgers lived at Pool House, one of the castle towers stood until 1795, when it was pulled down by the then owner Thomas Hornyold to provide materials for repairing the bridge at Upon-upon-Severn. Prior to this a house was built on part of the castle site. It was destroyed by fire in 1904 and has now itself vanished. In 1884 Mrs Lawson described how a considerable extent of the footings of the outer walls 2.7m thick had been exposed, unfortunately without any plan being made. An oven was also then visible and a number of domestic artifacts were found. All that now remains is a dry moat around a D-shaped platform about 90m by 70m.

HARTLEBURY CASTLE   SO 836713   O

Hartlebury was given to the bishops of Worcester by Burghred, King of Mercia. In the 1250s Bishop Walter de Cantilupe had a moat dug around the manor house and in 1268 Henry III licensed Bishop Giffard to build embattled walls and towers. Bishop Giffard entertained Edward I at Hartlebury in 1282 and provided military forces for the king's expedition into North Wales which culminated in the death of Welsh prince Llywelyn ap Gruffydd at Builth in that year.

In the mid 15th century Bishop Carpenter built a new gatehouse on the east side. Possibly this was the "keep", the last vestiges of which were removed by Bishop Hurd in 1781, although there are no signs of it on the Buck brothers print of 1731 which shows the east side much as it is now with gateway pavilions. Much of the walling of the great hall and the saloon at its south end also probably dates from the time of Bishop Carpenter, whilst the chapel, although much altered, may date from the last years of the 13th century. Leland described the castle in the 1530s as a "fayre Maner Place....having ii lytel towers covered with leade, and the chamber cauled the Bishop's Chamber also covered with leade, and there is a Chappell annexed to the said Chamber lykewyse covered with Leade, where is a lytell Bell weying by estimacion dimid hundred Weight. Also there is a Mote and a Ponde adjoyning to the said castell well stored with fyshe". About this time the castle became the principal residence of the bishops. It became their sole residence in 1846.

In 1644 King Charles' Commissioners of Array took refuge at the castle when pursued by Parliamentary troops. In 1646 William Sandys fortified the castle for the king, installing a garrison of 120 foot and 20 horse with provisions to last twelve months. In May of that year the castle was surrendered to Colonel Thomas Morgan after a two day siege. In 1647 the castle was sold to Thomas Westrowe for £3,133.6s.6d. and in 1648 it was used as a prison for incarcerating Royalist plotters. A survey then described it as a "strong castle situate upon a rock, with a moate around it full of water, which filleth several ponds stored with fish..." which suggests the walls were then still complete, but at some point during the period of the Cromwellian Protectorate the defences seem to have been dismantled.

Hartlebury Castle

Hartlebury Castle

The castle was eventually restored to the bishops and in 1675 Bishop Fleetwood began rebuilding the domestic apartments. Of this period are the whole of the NE wing, the central porch, the long gallery on the west side, and many windows and fireplaces serving the old rooms. In 1745 Bishop Maddox spent £1200 on remodelling the chapel. It was provided with a pretty fan vault designed by the architect Henry Keene, and a new set of windows with Y-tracery. Further work was carried out to the other rooms c1750-9, and the central lantern added, whilst between 1759 and 1774 Bishop Johnston refurnished the saloon and provided it with new gothic windows. In the 1780s Bishop Hurd had a library built over the long gallery and a westward facing bow window added. Bishop Yeatman Biggs turned the stable block into a college for clergy in 1905-18, and in 1964 the north wing and adjoining rooms were taken over by Worcestershire County Council and converted into the County Museum.

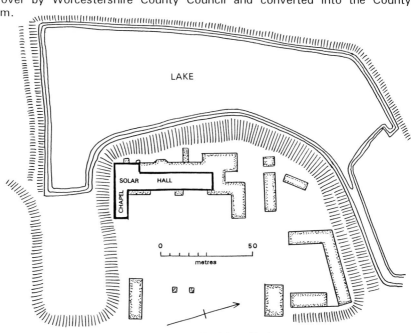

Plan of Hartlebury Castle

Holt Castle

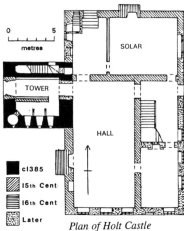

Plan of Holt Castle

HOLT CASTLE   SO 831626   V

Holt was held by Urse D'Abitot in 1086 and passed via his daughter to the Beauchamps. In the mid 13th century William Beauchamp gave Holt to his younger son John, and it is likely that a new manor house was built in that period. The oldest part of the existing building is a tower which is a relic of a house built by a John Beauchamp who was knighted and granted an estate in North Wales by Richard II in 1385. He was created Lord Beauchamp of Kidderminster in 1387, and, being one of King Richard's unpopular favourites, was executed by the Lords Appellants in 1388, and his honours declared forfeited. They were later restored to his son John, but forfeited again after Henry IV accession in 1399.

Holt passed to the Guise family in 1472 and was sold in 1557 to Sir John Bourn. He in turn sold it to Thomas Fortescue in 1578 and it was settled on his daughter Elizabeth and her husband Sir Thomas Bromley, then Lord Chancellor. The Croft family also had a part of the manor, but the whole was re-united under Henry Bromley, who died in 1615. Another Henry Bromley was made Lord Montfort in 1741. He sold Holt c1760 to Thomas, Lord Foley, later Earl of Dudley, and it remained with that family until the late 20th century.

The four storey tower measuring 7m by 7.7m externally was probably one of four standing at the corners of a rectangular main block, as at Broncroft Castle in Shropshire, built by Sir Simon Burley, another of Richard II's unpopular favourites executed in 1388, and the earlier house at Acton Burnell, also in Shropshire. Like these buildings the house at Holt would have been embattled and perhaps surrounded by a wet moat, now filled in, but the walls would have been thin and pierced with large windows, with defence taking second place to comfort. The whole building may never have been fully completed during the short period of John Beauchamp's ascendancy, and in the 15th century a new hall, probably smaller than the intended original, was built against the tower, in the basement of which an entrance passage was then made. North of the hall is a contemporary solar block which retains a number of original features, notable parts of the roof, although considerable further additions and alterations were made in the 16th and 18th centuries. In the latter period a service wing at the south end was removed.

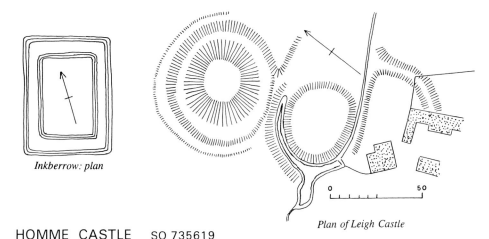

Inkberrow: plan

Plan of Leigh Castle

HOMME CASTLE   SO 735619

The farmhouse of Ham or Homme Castle may lie within an outer bailey of a small worn-down motte 3m high on a spur within a wide bend of the River Teme. A castle here is mentioned in 1207. Amongst the farmhouse outbuildings is a long brick vaulted cellar of the 17th or 18th century.

INKBERROW CASTLE   SP 017573

John Marshall, who died c1193, or his brother William, Earl of Pembroke, built a castle or fortified manor house at Inkberrow. In 1216 the Crown ordered William Cauntelow to provide wood to repair it. In 1231 King John's daughter Eleanor, widow of the second William Marshall, Earl of Pembroke, was allowed to reside in the castle, but in 1233, during the revolt of Richard Marshall, the castle was confiscated by Henry III, given to Baldwin de Lisle, and then later that year destroyed by the sheriff of Worcester. Inkberrow was later restored to Richard's brother Gilbert, who restocked the park there in 1234, and was evidently building a new residence in 1235. The house passed by marriage to the Monchelseys in 1241 and when they were forfeited as de Montfort supporters in 1265, Inkberrow went to William de Valence. From 1310 to 1389 it was held by the Hastings family. The house was a ruin in 1392. The rectangular wet moat east of the village centre marks the site.

LEIGH CASTLE   SO 781519

On a low lying site, probably once marshy, at Castle Green, 1km WSW of Bransford is an overgrown motte rising 6m from the bottom of the surrounding ditch with an outer bank to the west and north. The mount summit is a about 20m in diameter. To the south is a round bailey platform about 3m high and 40m across. Henry III took Leigh Castle from the rebel Hugh de Pembridge and gave it to Matthew de Gamages. Shortly after Hugh's death in 1272 his son recovered the estate, which was held from Pershore Abbey.

ROCHFORD MOTTE   SO 629685

Beside the River Teme north of Rochford Church is a worn down motte now about 2m high.

Moats at Strensham

SHRAWLEY CASTLE   SO 813655

The strong site of "Oliver's Mount" isolated by ditches on a sandstone ridge rising 15m above the River Severn on the east and a tributary valley on the west was excavated in 1928-30. There were traces of a rectangular court about 30m by 38m with octagonal corner towers and a square building in the middle of the east side which was destroyed by fire. The castle was probably built by the Le Poers c1300.

STRENSHAM CASTLE   SO 904405

James Russell was licensed to have an oratory at his house at Lower Strensham in 1283. He was then only a tenant but in 1298 he purchased the property. In 1388 Richard II licensed his Master of Horse, Sir John Russell, to crenellate the house. Sir William Russell was made a baronet by Charles in 1627 and served as the Royalist governor of Worcester during the Civil War. His seat at Strensham also appears to have served as a Royalist stronghold and seems to have been destroyed by Parliamentary forces as a consequence. At the Restoration Sir William built a new seat at Strensham Court. This in turn was entirely rebuilt in 1824.

No masonry remains standing of the medieval castle but behind Moat Farm is a platform measuring about 35m by 30m surrounded by a wet moat crossed by a wide causeway on the west side. About 15m beyond this moat is a concentric outer moat, also still full of water except for the southern half of the west side which was perhaps filled in when the building was destroyed. The area between the two moats, now rather overgrown, has a low bank with angular bastions at the corners, evidently a relic of when the castle was fortified in the 1640s for King Charles.

WOODMANTON MOAT   SO 718605   V

Edward III issued a licence to crenellate a house here in 1332. The timber-framed chapel and the fragment of a moat probably go back to that period. The chapel has a fine roof. In the 17th century an intermediate floor was inserted within it and either then or later the lower level became the farmhouse kitchen.

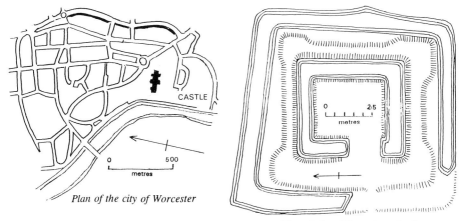

Plan of the city of Worcester

Plan of site of Strensham Castle

WORCESTER CASTLE   SO 849547

In 1069 Urse D'Abitot, Sheriff of Worcestershire, greatly annoyed Ealdred, former Bishop of Worcester and now Bishop of York, by cutting off part of the cemetery of the cathedral-priory at Worcester for the outer defences of a newly built motte and bailey castle. The motte, which was finally removed in 1848, lay beside the River Severn and rose 24m above its east bank. An inner bailey lay to the east and to the north, on the site now occupied by College Green, was the outer bailey. The Beauchamp family, as hereditary sheriffs of Worcester, held the castle throughout the 12th century. The wooden buildings were destroyed in 1113 during the first of three fires to break out in the city of Worcester during the 12th century. They were soon rebuilt, probably again in wood, and the motte, tower, gateway, bridge, bailey palisade, hall, chambers and the cellars of the king's houses within the castle are all mentioned in the sheriff's accounts during the reigns of Henry II and Richard I. The expenditure recorded is fairly modest and probably only refers to repairs. In 1204 King John, who frequently visited the city, and was buried in Worcester Cathedral in 1216, ordered the sheriff to rebuild the wooden gatehouse in stone, which was done at a cost of £40. In the conflict between John and his barons at the end of his reign the castle was held by William Marshall the younger against the king and was attacked by the Earl of Chester and Faulkes de Breaute.

Just after King John's death the monks of the cathedral-priory petitioned Henry III for the ground taken by Urse D'Abitot in 1069 to be returned to them. The young king agreed to this and the two baileys were then given to the monks whilst the motte and its tower remained in the custody of Walter de Beauchamp. By this time the castle at Elmley had became the principal Beauchamp seat and no further interest was taken in the dismembered castle at Worcester either by the sheriff or the king. When Robert de Ferrers, Earl of Derby, entered and sacked the city in 1263 in support of Simon de Montfort, it was "through the old castle" indicating that it was then untenable and disused. The Beauchamps and their successors maintained some interest in the land until 1487, when it was surrendered to Henry VII by Anne, Countess of Warwick. Leland describes the castle as "clene down" and says that "half the base courte or area of it is now within the waulle of the close of the cathedrall churche". For many years the county prison stood on the other half of the site until transferred elsewhere in 1809. A map of 1741 shows not only the motte but also the southern rampart of the former inner bailey as then still existing.

The city of Worcester was a Roman fortress probably established in the first century AD and refortified later. Fresh defences were constructed in 899 against the Danes by Aethelred, Earl of Mercia. Worcester received a royal charter in 1189, and in the early 13th century Henry allowed the townsfolk to make tolls to pay for building the stone walls which stood complete until the 18th century. Of these there now remain just several low lengths on the east side with a small round turret and a battered plinth but no other features of interest. A fortified gateway stood upon the 14th century bridge over the Severn replaced in 1781. There were six other gateways, namely the Water Gate near the river on the NW, the Fore Gate on the north, St Martin's Gate and Friars' Gate on the east, Sidbury Gate on the SE, and Frog Gate on the south. They were destroyed in the late 18th century because their narrow archways restricted traffic flows. The last to remain was St Martin's Gate, which had two octagonal towers flanking the outer portal and three parallel gables facing the city. The Sidbury Gate had round flanking towers, the base of the northern one being uncovered in 1908. Excavations have shown that outside the walls was a flat-bottomed water-filled ditch 12m wide. Towards the end of 1642 Worcester was occupied by a Parliamentary army under the Earl of Essex but throughout most of the Civil War the city was a Royalist stronghold. It withstood an attack by Sir William Waller in 1643 and finally surrendered in July 1646. The worn down bastioned fortlet commanding the site of the Sidbury Gate is a relic of the Commonwealth period, when the city's loyalty to the Protectorate was in doubt.

WORCESTER PALACE   SO 849546

The former bishop's palace, which became the deanery in 1842, lies to the north of the cathedral. Externally most of it dates from the time of Bishop Hough,, 1717-43, and Bishop Johnston, 1759-74, who spent over £5,000 on additions, but within it are various vaulted undercrofts of the 13th century. They probably date from the time of Bishop Giffard, who was licensed to crenellate the palace in 1271. The two acre precinct may have been surrounded by a high embattled wall with a substantial gatehouse, but the various buildings within it appear to have been purely domestic in nature. The undercrofts formed part of the bishop's hall and chapel and it is thought that there was once a large great hall to the south. Also incorporated are some featureless 12th century walls.

Turret on Worcester city wall

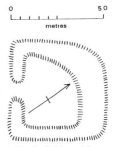

0   50
metres

Pendock Moor Moat

LIST OF MOATED SITES IN WORCESTERSHIRE

ABBOTS MORTON SP 026551 A dry moat lies by a house in the village.
ASTWOOD COURT SP 032623 An oval wet moat surrounds the house.
BANNALS FARM SO 644637 A fragment of a moat lies beside the house.
BENTLEY SO 989664 A rectangular wet moat lies in a field.
BIRTSMORTON COURT SO 801355 Fine example of a wet moated house.
BLACKGREVES SP 066755 A rectangular moat surrounds the farmhouse.
BOWERCOURT SO 736707 Part of a wet moat lies by the farm.
CHURCHILL SO 923536 Part of a moat lies near the church.
CORSE LAWN SO 824304 A wedge-shaped moat lies in fields.
COTHERIDGE SO 775557 A dry moat surrounds Moat Cottage.
CROOKBARROW HILL SO 876524 Part of a wet moat lies by a house.
CROWLE SO 922559 A dry fragment of a moat lies near the church.
DUNSTALL SO 883427 Two arms of a wet moat lie beside a house.
EARLS CROOME SO 873420 Rectangular platform in partly wet moat.
EARDISTON SO 696681 Part of a moat lies beside Moor Farm.
ELMLEY CASTLE SO 985402 Two arms of wet moat in field east of castle.
FAIRFIELD SO 946758 Deep dry moat around garden of house.
FECKENHAM SP 008615 An earthwork lies in a field by the village.
GANNOW GREEN SO 984784 A rectangular moat lies in a field.
HANLEY SWAN SO 814435 Part of a wet moat lies beside a stream.
HARDWICK GREEN SO 817327 Three sides of a wet moat beside a farm.
HARVINGTON SO 877745 An irregularly shaped moat surrounds the hall.
HILL CROOME SO 885409 Part of a wet moat lies beside Manor Farm.
HOLBERROW GREEN SP 013597 Rectangular moat by house. 2nd moat nearby.
HUDDINGTON COURT SO 944573 Rectangular moat lies around the house.
HUNNINGTON SO 963812 Three sides of a moat lie in a field.
LONGDON SO 839361 Two arms of a wet moat lie beside a house.
LULSLEY SO 746555 A rectangular wet moat lies beside a house.
MADRESFIELD SO 809474 Three sides of a wet moat surround the house.
MOON'S MOAT SP 069682 Three sides of a wet moat lie in a field.
MOORGREEN HALL SP 054743 A dry rectangular moat lies in a field.
MORTON UNDERHILL SP 013591 Just a pool now remains beside a house.
NAUNTON BEAUCHAMP SO 959523 A dry moat lies in a field.
NORTON SO 872515 Two arms of a wet moat remain near the barracks.
PENDOCK MOOR SO 814348 A dry rectangular moat lies in a field.
PIGEON HOUSE FARM SO 810312 Two arms of a wet moat beside a farm.
PRIORY FARM SP 053573 An oval wet moat lies beside the farm.
ROCHFORD SO 634673 Rectangular moat.
ROCK SO 733710 A partly wet moat lies south of the church.
ROUS LENCH SP 016533 Rectangular dry moat in field by church.
SHERRARDS GREEN SO 798462 Rectangular wet moat around farm.
SHURNOCK SP 027608 Three arms of a moat remain by the house.
SODINGTON HALL SO 693709 A fragment of a moat lies by the farm.
STOCK WOOD SP 003591 Three arms of a moat remain by the house.
SUCKLEY COURT SO 714514 Fragments of a wet moat lie beside a farm.
TANNERS GREEN SP 088744 Fragments of a moat lie in fields.
THE ELMS SO 796574 An oval wet moat lies in fields.
THROCKMORTON SO 982499 Square wet moat by church. Other moats nearby.
TOOKEYS FARM SP 040618 Part of a wet moat remains by the house.
WARNDON SO 888577 House beside church still has a moat.
WHITE LADIES ASTON SO 925521 Three sides of a wet moat by house.
WOODEND FARM SO 777574 Two arms of a wet moat lie beside farm.

GLOSSARY OF TERMS

APSE - Semi-circular or polygonal shaped structure. ASHLAR - Masonry of blocks with even faces and square edges. BAILEY - Defensible court enclosed by a wall or a palisade and ditch. BARBICAN - Defensible court, passage or porch in front of an entrance. BASTION - A projection rising no higher than the curtain wall. BATTER - The inward inclination of a wall face. CRENEL - A cut-away part of a parapet. CORBEL - A projecting bracket to support other stonework or a timber beam. CURTAIN WALL - A high enclosing stone wall around a bailey. HOARDING - Wooden gallery at a wall top providing machicolations. JAMB - A side of a doorway, window or other opening. KEEP - A citadel or ultimate strongpoint. The term is not medieval and such towers were then called donjons, from which word is derived the word dungeon meaning a prison. LIGHT - A compartment of a window. LOOP - A small opening to admit light or for the discharge of missiles. MACHICOLATION - A slot for dropping or firing missiles at assailants. MERLONS - The upstanding portions of a parapet. MOAT - A defensive ditch, water filled or dry. MOTTE - A steep sided flat-topped mound, partly or wholly man-made. MULLION - A vertical member dividing the lights of a window. PARAPET -A wall for protection at any sudden drop. PISCINA - Stone basin for washing out holy veseels after mass. PLINTH - The projecting base of a wall. It may be battered (sloped) or stepped. PORTCULLIS - A wooden gate made to rise and fall in vertical grooves, being hoisted by a windlass above. POSTERN - A back entrance or lesser gateway. RINGWORK - An embanked enclosure of more modest size than a bailey, generally of greater width but less elevated than a motte summit. ROLL MOULDING - Moulding of D-shaped section. SHELL KEEP - A small stone walled court built upon a motte or ringwork. SOLAR - A private living room for the lord and his family. STRONGHOUSE - An unfortified mansion not easy to break into or burn down because of its solid walls and moat. WALL-WALK - A walkway on top of a wall, protected by a parapet. WARD - A stone walled defensive enclosure.

PUBLIC ACCESS TO THE SITES   Codes used in the gazetteers.

E Buildings in the care of English Heritage. Fee payable at some sites.

F Sites to which there is free access at any time.

H Buildings currently used as hotels, restaurants, shops (free access to outside).

O Buildings opened to the public by private owners, local councils, National Trust.

V Buildings closely visible from public roads, paths, churchyards & open spaces.

FURTHER READING

Herefordshire, Buildings of England series, Nikolaus Pevsner, 1963
Worcestershire, Buildings of England series, Nickolaus Pevsner, 1968
Victoria County History of Herefordshire (Several volumes, various dates)
Victoria County History of Worcestershire (Several volumes, various dates)
Royal Commission on Historical Monuments Inventory for Herefordshire (3 vols)
A History of the Castles of Herefordshire, C.Robinson, 1869
A History of The Mansions & Manors of Herefordshire, C.Robinson, 1873
Herefordshire Under Arms, Charles Hopkinson, 1985
Herefordshire Castles. A List of Classified Sites, Roger Stirling-Brown
A History of Herefordshire, John & Margaret West, 1985
Annual Transactions of the Woolhope Naturalists Field Club
Norman Castles in Britain, Derek Renn, 1968   Herefordshire Archeological News
Hanley Castle.....Heart of Malvern Chase, Pamela Hurle, 1978
Castles & Moated Sites of Herefordshire, Ron Shoesmith, 1996